THE G[...]
IN NEW[...]

GENERAL EDIT[...]
Pe[...]

Sophocles.
Aias =

SOPHOCLES: Aias

SOPHOCLES

Aias
[Ajax]

Translated by
HERBERT GOLDER
and
RICHARD PEVEAR

New York   Oxford
OXFORD UNIVERSITY PRESS
1999

Oxford University Press

Oxford   New York
Athens   Auckland   Bangkok   Bogotá   Buenos Aires
Calcutta   Cape Town   Chennai   Dar es Salaam   Delhi   Florence
Hong Kong   Istanbul   Karachi   Kuala Lumpur   Madrid   Melbourne
Mexico City   Mumbai   Nairobi   Paris   São Paulo   Singapore
Taipei   Tokyo   Toronto   Warsaw

and associated companies in
Berlin   Ibadan

Published by Oxford University Press, Inc.
198 Madison Avenue, New York, New York 10016

Oxford is a registered trademark of Oxford University Press, Inc.

Library of Congress Cataloging-in-Publication Data
Sophocles.
[Ajax. English]
Aias / translated by Herbert Golder and Richard Pevear.
p.   cm. — (Greek tragedy in new translations)
    978-0-19-512819-2
1. Ajax (Greek mythology) — Drama.   I. Title.   II. Series.
PA4414.A5G65   1998   882'.01 — dc21
98-24421

98765
Printed in the United States of America

EDITORS' FOREWORD

"*The Greek Tragedy in New Translations* is based on the conviction that poets like Aeschylus, Sophocles, and Euripides can only be properly rendered by translators who are themselves poets. Scholars may, it is true, produce useful and perceptive versions. But our most urgent present need is for a *re-creation* of these plays—as though they had been written, freshly and greatly, by masters fully at home in the English of our own times."

With these words, the late William Arrowsmith announced the purpose of this series, and we intend to honor that purpose. As was true of most of the volumes that began to appear in the 1970s—first under Arrowsmith's editorship, later in association with Herbert Golder—those for which we bear editorial responsibility are products of close collaboration between poets and scholars. We believe (as Arrowsmith did) that the skills of both are required for the difficult and delicate task of transplanting these magnificent specimens of another culture into the soil of our own place and time, to do justice both to their deep differences from our patterns of thought and expression and to their palpable closeness to our most intimate concerns. Above all, we are eager to offer contemporary readers dramatic poems that convey as vividly and directly as possible the splendor of language, the complexity of image and idea, and the intensity of emotion of the originals. This entails, among much else, the recognition that the tragedies were meant for performance—as scripts for actors—to be sung and danced as well as spoken. It demands writing of inventiveness, clarity, musicality, and dramatic power. By such standards we ask that these translations be judged.

This series is also distinguished by its recognition of the need of nonspecialist readers for a critical introduction informed by the best recent scholarship, but written clearly and without condescension. Each play is followed by notes designed not only to elucidate obscure references but also to mediate the conventions of the Athenian stage as well as those features of the Greek text that might otherwise go unnoticed. The notes are supplemented by a glossary of mythical and geographical terms that should make it possible to read the play without turning elsewhere for basic information. Stage directions are sufficiently ample to aid readers in imagining the action as they read. Our fondest hope, of course, is that these versions will be staged not only in the minds of their readers but also in the theaters to which, after so many centuries, they still belong.

A NOTE ON THE SERIES FORMAT

If only for the illusion of coherence, a series of thirty-three Greek plays requires a consistent format. Different translators, each with an individual voice, cannot possibly develop the sense of a single coherent style for each of the three tragedians; nor even the illusion that, despite their differences, the tragedians share a common set of conventions and a generic, or period, style. But they can at least share a common approach to orthography and a common vocabulary of conventions.

1. *Spelling of Greek names*

Adherence to the old convention whereby Greek names were first Latinized before being housed in English is gradually disappearing. We are now clearly moving away from Latinization and toward precise transliteration. The break with tradition may be regrettable, but there is much to be said for hearing and seeing Greek names as though they were both Greek and *new*, instead of Roman or neo-classical importations. We cannot of course see them as wholly new. For better or worse certain names and myths are too deeply rooted in our literature and thought to be dislodged. To speak of "Helene" and "Hekabe" would be no less pedantic and absurd than to write "Aischylos" or "Platon" or "Thoukydides." These are of course borderline cases. "Jocasta" (as opposed to "Iokaste") is not a major mythical figure in her own right; her familiarity in her Latin form is a function of the fame of Sophocles' play as the tragedy *par excellence*. And as tourists we go to Delphi, not Delphoi. The precisely transliterated form may be pedantically "right," but the pedantry goes against the grain of cultural habit and actual usage.

As a general rule, we have therefore adopted a "mixed" orthography according to the principles suggested above. When a name has been firmly housed in English (admittedly the question of domestication is often moot), the traditional spelling has been kept. Otherwise names have been transliterated. Throughout the series the *-os* termination of masculine names has been adopted, and Greek diphthongs (as in Iphi-gene*ia*) have normally been retained. We cannot expect complete agreement from readers (or from translators, for that matter) about borderline cases. But we want at least to make the operative principle clear: to walk a narrow line between orthographical extremes in the hope of keeping what should not, if possible, be lost; and refreshing, in however tenuous a way, the specific sound and name-boundedness of Greek experience.

2. Stage directions

The ancient manuscripts of the Greek plays do not supply stage directions (though the ancient commentators often provide information relevant to staging, delivery, "blocking," etc.). Hence stage directions must be inferred from words and situations and our knowledge of Greek theatrical conventions. At best this is a ticklish and uncertain procedure. But it is surely preferable that good stage directions should be provided by the translator than that readers should be left to their own devices in visualizing action, gesture, and spectacle. Obviously the directions supplied should be both spare and defensible. Ancient tragedy was austere and "distanced" by means of masks, which means that the reader must not expect the detailed intimacy ("He shrugs and turns wearily away," "She speaks with deliberate slowness, as though to emphasize the point," etc.) that characterizes stage directions in modern naturalistic drama.

3. Numbering of lines

For the convenience of the reader who may wish to check the English against the Greek text or vice versa, the lines have been numbered according to both the Greek text and the translation. The lines of the English translation have been numbered in multiples of ten, and these numbers have been set in the right-hand margin. The notes that follow the text have been keyed to the line numbers of the translation. The (inclusive) Greek numeration will be found bracketed at the top of the page. Readers will doubtless note that in many plays the English lines outnumber the Greek, but they should not therefore conclude that the translator has been unduly prolix. In most cases the reason is simply that the translator has adopted the free-flowing norms of modern Anglo-American prosody, with its brief, breath- and emphasis-determined lines, and its habit of indicating cadence and caesuras by line length and setting rather than by conventional punctuation. Other translators have preferred four-beat or five-beat lines, and in these cases Greek and English numerations will tend to converge.

Durham, N.C.
Chapel Hill, N.C.
1998

Peter Burian
Alan Shapiro

CONTENTS

Introduction, 3

On the Translation, 23

Characters, 26

Aias, 27

Notes on the Text, 81

Glossary, 95

AIAS

INTRODUCTION

"The ancient simplicity into which honor so largely entered was laughed down and disappeared," wrote Thucydides (3.83), describing the moral decline of the late fifth century B.C. That same judgment might equally well be applied to the story of the Homeric warrior Aias, whose betrayal and tragic suicide embodies the final eclipse of ancient honor itself. In the arts of war and in sheer magnificence, Aias, Homer's "bulwark of the Achaians," was second only to Achilles. By rights, after Achilles died, his armor, the highest prize of honor, was owed to Aias. But the Greeks denied Aias his due, awarding the arms instead to the wily Odysseus. To Aias, the man of action, that *his* prize should be given to Odysseus, the man of words, was intolerable. Outraged and humiliated, noble Aias did as his honor demanded, dying on his own sword.

Sophocles inherited an Aias tradition from Homer's *Iliad* and other epic poems. Aeschylus and Pindar, Sophocles' older contemporaries, had also presented versions of Aias' story. Together, these versions create the convention against which Sophocles shaped his own radically different Aias. But Sophocles' concept of heroism is also deeply rooted in the tragic heroism of Homer's *Iliad*. "Always to be best" (*aien aristeuein*) was the charge given to Achilles, Homer's greatest hero—the epitome of epic heroism. To the modern ear this may perhaps sound like mere competitive egoism. But "being best" (*aristos*) in Homer meant rather a *striving* for excellence or *arete*, a suprapersonal ideal pursued without compromise, even at the cost of life itself. In his first speech, Sophocles' Aias sounds the Homeric note: "Honor in life / or in death: if a man is born noble, / he must have one or the other" (530–32). Thus the hero dies as he lives—absolutely. The stress is on the manner, not merely the matter, of living and dying. The word *aristos* ("best") in Greek is clearly related to the word *arete*, usually translated as "excellence." But *arete* is not merely an ethical term. It is above all a quality of character, to be realized only in action, by active fulfillment of one's *daimon*, or "indwelling destiny." "Character," said Heraclitus, "*is* destiny." Sophoclean tragedy explores and dramatizes this dynamic; character emerges through the act, or agony, of becoming. And, at a certain point, action becomes fatal, revealing, finally, the hero's destiny. The hero is therefore involved in a great struggle with his *daimon* "to become the thing he is," to adapt Pindar's noble phrase. Sophocles inherited this concept of heroic *arete*, in which character and destiny are one. But, in the case of Aias, the identity of character and destiny seems conspicuously absent: Aias, the man of honor, dies in shame. This paradox is at the heart of Sophocles' play. But only in the context of the received traditions can the full import of the Sophoclean Aias' "fatal" act be revealed.

Homer's Aias exemplifies ancient honor almost as much as Achilles himself. A giant of a man, famous for tenacity and valor rather than eloquence, Aias seems at first sight an Achilles manqué—the inarticulate man of action. But Achilles and Aias represent two complementary, tragic types; together they provide a fuller sense of the tragic hero than either hero alone. Achilles was passionately volatile and famous for swiftness, which made him deadly, especially on the attack. Aias, in contrast, was the steady, immovable defender; his colossal size and obdurate relentlessness made him quite literally the "bulwark of the Achaians." Each had his unique *daimon*, which disclosed his essential character through his acts. By inactivity, Achilles resisted his *daimon*; he is less than himself when he sits idly on the beach and talks of returning home to a long, inglorious life. By the same token, Aias, when forced by Zeus to retreat, ceases to be Aias:

> But Zeus on high drove fear upon Aias so that he stood
> amazed *and threw the seven layered, oxhide shield behind him*,
> terror in his eyes, he glared all around like a cornered beast
> and backed up slowly, turning this way and that like a fiery lion
> beaten back from the cattle-yard by dogs and farmers,
>   . . . furious but afraid
> Aias retreated from the Trojans, *his heart sinking, much unwilling . . .*
> *hard to move as a mule* in a cornfield, who stays feeding
> though beaten with sticks . . ."
>
>   (*Iliad* 11.544–61)

Though peerless in war, Aias loses three times in the games at Patroklos' funeral. He is, by nature, too inflexible to play "games." He is most himself when most serious—in mortal combat with Hektor, or when he single-handedly drives off the Trojans from Patroklos' body, or prevents the enemy from firing the ships. Standing firm against a worthy adversary or impossible odds is the real genius of Aias:

> . . . holding back the Trojans, *as a timbered rock ridge*
> *holds back water*, one stretching the length of a plain,
> with flooding currents from strong rivers pounding against it,
> still holding and beating the waters right back across the plain,
> no wave having nearly strength enough to break it,
> *so the two Aiases held off the attacking Trojans forever.*
>
> (*Iliad* 17.747–53)

To move unmoving Aias is to change him: the mountain ceases to be mountain if it moves. But for both unbending Aias and swift-footed Achilles, a defining strength is also a fatal weakness.

Each man suffers a different temporal tragedy. Achilles is "swift-footed," but the intensity with which he fights and lives ensures that he will be "swift-fated"; his life will be brief. Aias, the immovable man of honor, is instead bound to outlive his world, to see it change and time pass him by. He is not "a man for all seasons." Achilles is at least spared the pathos of living on in an unheroic age. But Aias lives to see his heroic labors come to nothing. His tragedy, however, is not simply that of individual obsolescence, but also that of a society that sacrifices its highest ideals of honor and nobility to expediency. The expedient Odysseus is the canny and flexible opportunist, Homer's "man of many turns"; his *arete* is an ability to adapt, to change with the times. No hero was more strikingly different from both Achilles and Aias. "As the gates of Hades," says Achilles to Odysseus (*Iliad* 9.312–13), "I hate the man who hides one thing in his heart and says another." But to Aias, who has spoken bluntly of honor and friendship, Achilles replies, "You have spoken, Aias, like a man after my own heart" (*Iliad* 9.645).

Homer does not tell us how Aias fell. Epic poems, lost to us but known to Sophocles' audience, narrated the grisly sequence of events. Like Aeschylus and Pindar before him, Sophocles was free to adapt this story as he chose, counting on his audience's familiarity with the mythical variants. By emphasizing, omitting, or innovating, the poet could use a myth to express his own vision. No spectator would fail to notice variations on stories known by heart; the poet knew what his audience knew and therefore what that audience might expect. The conventions, established by previous treatments of Aias' suicide, created the expectations with which, and against which, Sophocles wrote.

From fragments the episodes of the epic cycle can be pieced together. A quarrel arose between Aias and Odysseus over Achilles' arms;

unable to choose between them, the Greeks asked Trojan prisoners to judge. Though accounts vary, the supple talker and thinker, Odysseus, prevailed. Shamed by defeat, Aias disappeared into his tent to die, "blameless" in Greek eyes; later, he was given a hero's funeral. In still another version, Aias' rage turns to madness, which leads in turn to suicide. In yet another—the one employed by Sophocles here—Aias went mad and slaughtered the Greek livestock before taking his own life; for this, he was denied a hero's burial. In presenting an Aias drama, Sophocles could choose from a number of potentially dramatic accounts and a variety of interpretations. All the variants raise questions about the three aspects of the myth that Sophocles chose to confront directly: madness, suicide, and burial. Precisely these elements determine whether Aias is to be considered heroic, and in what sense. The verdict is moot, and Sophocles therefore free to explore what meaning he might find among the various Aias legends.

Aeschylus had already offered a comprehensive interpretation of the legend. His Aias trilogy presented a sequence of events that suggest a heroic, even divine, Aias, and that moral progression that characterizes Aeschylean theater. In Sophocles the suicide is the dead center of a single play, overshadowing everything else; in Aeschylus the suicide was only one of three equally significant theatrical events—the debate, the suicide, and the establishment of Aias' hero-cult on the Athenian island of Salamis. Like the *Oresteia*, the trilogy exhibited a redemptive pattern: Aias' anger was the "Fury" that, in the final play, was redeemed. Far from being the center of the trilogy, the suicide and events preceding it were not dramatized at all but reported by an eyewitness. A curious mythical variant regarding the hero's invulnerability was also introduced. When, bent on suicide, Aias failed to find the vulnerable point, a god appeared to aid him. He died, in other words, befriended by heaven and nearly godlike in his invulnerability. Finally, in the last play, Aias' death was revealed as part of a more universal scheme. And since both Salamis and Aias were "Athenian," Aeschylus' dramatic portrayal of Aias enshrined upon Salamis surely redounded to the glory of Athens herself.[1]

But to the Theban aristocrat Pindar, the death of Aias represented the end of the heroic age. Indifferent, even hostile, to Aeschylus' cosmic optimism, Pindar presented an Aias whose loss irreversibly diminished the world. Greece had betrayed its own greatness when it abandoned noble Aias in favor of crafty Odysseus. Pindar, moreover,

---

1. The three plays were *The Award of the Arms*, frg. 174–78aN, *The Women of Thrace* frg. 83N, and *The Women of Salamis* frg. 216N. My reconstruction of this trilogy is of course conjectural.

injected an anachronistic political meaning into his treatment of the myth, linking Aias not to Salamis (and Athens) but to his favorite city, Aigina, a bastion of conservative, aristocratic Greece (and perhaps no less important, the enemy of Athens). Having been betrayed by its ally Sparta, Aigina now "belonged" to Athens. So it is tempting to see in Pindar's ode, composed for an Aiginetan victor at the Nemean games, an equation between the defeat of this "unAthenian" Aias and that of Pindar's city of heroes—a victory of immoral intelligence, that famous "Attic cleverness," over honor:

> Envy's fang bit into the flesh of Aias and twisting inside
> ran him through with a sword.
> Strong—even in silence—he is eclipsed by that hateful fight,
> the greatest prize given for the flashy lie,
> the Greeks flattering Odysseus, their secret ballot leaving
> Aias stripped of the golden arms, alone
> to wrestle with death.
>
> But the winner was no match for Aias at ripping
> wounds in warm flesh, when his long spear
> was their only shield in the fight that raged
> over Achilles' body, or in a thousand other struggles
> in those days of too much dying.
> Despicable, even then, the art of guile
> —weaving webs of words, twisting thoughts, casting blame,
> working to no good end—drives splendor into darkness
> and honors the obscure, holding up a glory
> rotten to the root.

(Nemean 8.23–34)

To this vividly implicit condemnation of Athens, Sophocles responds by immediately, in the first scene, rehabilitating Pindar's villain, Odysseus. But by isolating Aias, by focusing solely on the suicide, and finally by suppressing the confident Aeschylean coda, Sophocles also refuses Aeschylus' optimistic marriage of the divine hero with Athens. Everything essential to Sophocles' interpretation, moreover, has been condensed into a single play, and the suicide is the midpoint climax to which it builds. Thereafter Aias' huge corpse dominates the stage.

But dramatizing Aias' suicide creates genuine problems for an Athenian playwright passionately concerned, like Sophocles, with human greatness. There was simply no precedent for heroic suicide. For Greek males, suicide was, unlike the *seppuku* of the Japanese samurai, not an honorable death. Under extreme circumstances, heroes might long for death; and while they often chose courses of action that led to death, they never took their own lives. Suicide was a desperate act, restricted in tragedy solely to women. Far from confirming heroism, Aias' suicide in fact marks the end of the heroic tradition, just as the victory of Odysseus signals the beginning of a new and less heroic age.

In Athens, where Aias was the eponymous hero of one of the ten tribes, suicide may have raised moral questions. His statue, paid divine honors, stood prominently in the marketplace, and clans claiming descent from Aias were among the city's most illustrious citizens. "Divine" Aias was honored by all of Greece, along with Poseidon and Athene, for his tutelary role in the Greek victory over Persia at Salamis in 480 B.C. Athens was justly proud of its link to the deified hero and its role as savior of Greece. Hence, the ignominy of Aias' suicide was hardly the most propitious subject for artistic representation; and in Attic art generally, it is Aias' military prowess, not his suicide, that is emphasized. So we can be reasonably certain that Sophocles' insistent, dramatic focus on the "forbidden" subject must have surprised his audience, violating, as it did, their expectations.

Still more surprising is the characterization of Aias as eloquent and reflective. The Homeric ideal as embodied by Achilles was excellence in both word and deed. But the Homeric Aias is clearly lacking in eloquence and mental agility. A staunch defender, he is never depicted as a strategist, nor does he participate, like the other heroes, in the councils of the chieftains. At one point, his tenacity in battle is compared to that of an ox (*Iliad* 13.703 ff.), a comparison invidiously "recalled" by Agamemnon in this play ("An ox, for all / its great girth, is driven down the road / with a little whip" [1403–5]); elsewhere, his steadfastness invites comparison with a stubborn ass (cited above). His great size and simplicity helped to create the traditional image of the hulking brute. Even in death, in his sublime Homeric moment, Aias is famous for what Longinus called his "eloquent silence": the refusal of his shade to speak to Odysseus in Hades. By contrast, the Sophoclean Aias dominates the stage, not only with his imposing presence, but with four of the most remarkable speeches in drama. One must go to Shakespeare—to Richard II's prison monologue or Macbeth's "brief candle" speech or even Hamlet's "to be or not to be"—to find anything like Aias' prodigious speech on time (712 ff.). These are lines, Bernard Knox writes, "so majestic, remote and mysterious, and at the same time so passionate, dramatic, and complex, that if this were all that had survived of Sophocles he would still have to be reckoned as one of the world's greatest poets."[2] The profound novelty of this eloquent and deadly lucid Aias is absolutely crucial to the reader's understanding of the play.

2. Bernard Knox, "The *Ajax* of Sophocles," *Word and Action: Essays on the Ancient Greek Theater*

II

The great Sophoclean Aias emerges in his confrontation with death. Through the speeches that arise from that confrontation he comes into being. It is his reflections and the transforming urgency of his rhetoric that make his suicide wholly unconventional in its metaphysical resonance. The hero's deftly paced and penetrating words detach him completely from the ignominy traditionally associated with his death; at the same time, they give his suicide a meaning radically different from that of the Aeschylean apotheosis. This Aias is neither the deified hero of Athenian cult nor the archaic warrior who dies in shame—not the hero whom time has passed by, but rather the *man* who steps beyond time.

Sophocles begins his play, however, with the familiar figure of Aias disgraced. Exploiting the most sensational version of Aias' fall, the dramatist presents an Aias at the extreme epic end. His audacious words and savagery seem brutish simplicity beside the humane Odysseus, whose vision of human transience ("we who live / are all phantoms, fleeting shadows," [151–52]) makes him sound more like Pindar himself ("Creatures of a day. What is man? What is he not? Man / shadow of a dream" *Pythian* 8.95) than the immoral schemer of *Nemean* 8 ("twisting thoughts, casting blame, working to no good end"). Timeless Greek wisdom stands behind Odysseus' compassionate humility, whereas Aias is tainted by horror and a blood-lust fueled by violent hatred, Homeric self-assertion taken to a murderous extreme. Smeared from head to toe with the gore of his animal victims, mad Aias visibly confirms the death throes of Homeric heroism. Worse still, if Athene had not deterred him and driven him mad, he would have been soaked with human blood. This dark and savage project of murdering the Greeks in the night is Sophocles' own invention. The Aias of the *Iliad* had moved in the light, preferring death in light to life in darkness: "Father Zeus," he once cried in battle,

> remove us from darkness, let our eyes see bright aether,
> and then destroy us in shining daylight,
> since this is now your pleasure.

> (*Iliad* 17.645 ff.)

Sophocles' Aias himself has become a vision of darkness. The sight of him conjures up "phantoms" and "fleeting shadows" before Odysseus'

(The Johns Hopkins University Press, 1979), p. 125. Reprinted from *Harvard Studies in Classical Philology* 65 (1961).

eyes; and "Darkness, my light! / brightest gloom" (430 f.) is Aias' own vision when he wakes from madness. The archaic warrior seems now an avatar from some dark and brutish past, more like a pre- than a post-Homeric memory. He could not be more degraded, more ludicrously absurd.

Tekmessa's description of the night's events only darkens the initial image; she reports Aias' insane joy in inflicting torture, breaking necks, and flaying victims alive. The worst, she warns, is yet to come. The following scene does little to mitigate her forebodings and our revulsion: "sprawled / in the wreck of his fate" (351 f.), a saner Aias is wheeled out into view on the trundle stage, the *ekkyklema* — but nothing has changed except that his delusions are gone, replaced by his fatal shame. Aias still hates the Greeks; his only regret is that his hand missed its true target. Even when he is allowed to recall something of his former Homeric greatness ("Skamander, river / hostile to the Greeks, / there is one man your water / will not mirror / again—I will have / my full say—a man / like none Troy ever set eyes on . . ." [455–61]), the spectacle of the hero-butcher overwhelms us, intensifying his dreadful fall.

But here, at Aias's lowest point, his transformation begins. No tragic characters sink lower, or rise higher, than those of Sophocles. Their savage degradation is vividly depicted — Philoktetes' oozing wound, Oedipus' bleeding eyes, Herakles' pain-racked body — in order to intensify their godlike struggle against that degradation. Disgraced, drenched in animal blood, victim of his own brutality, Aias discovers his agony as a mortal. He now knows his true fate: his name, *Aias* (from *aiadzein*, "to cry in pain" [468 ff.]), *is* his destiny. Aias stands before us polluted with gore; but this brute blood is tragic confirmation that he too is a creature of blood — mortal, born to die and therefore to cry *aiai*.

The anguished cry *aiai*, which begins Aias' speech (468 ff.), and the heroic finale "Honor in life, / or in death" (530 f.) express the range of his character; beyond this, as Aias concludes, "You've heard all there is to say" (533). The outcry and the avowal of silence frame Aias' lament for a greatness the world has lost. We get a hint of what he might have become, if the world had not changed: a man like his father, Telamon, shipmate of Herakles and sacker of Troy, who sailed home with the highest prize of honor. But dishonored now, Aias can never return to face such a father. A shadow of his Homeric self, surviving in a world that has outlived his kind of *arete*, Aias sees that the only heroism left him is the essential human achievement — dignity in dying, "some act that will prove / [his] nature" (520 f.). This is the man the world has lost:

> To stretch your life out when you see
> that nothing can break its misery
> is shameful — day after day
> moving forward or back from the end line
> of death.
>
> (523–27)

Though diminished by the changing world he abhors, enough of Aias is left for him to speak like the hero who led the fight against Troy:

> Better all at once to take our chances at living or dying,
> than be worn away slowly by the dreadful slaughter . . .
> (*Iliad* 15.511 f.)

Even his farewell to Tekmessa and Eurysakes pointedly recalls the famous Homeric scene of Hektor's farewell to Andromache and their son (*Iliad* 6.390 ff.). Hektor hears words from Andromache remarkably like those of Tekmessa here; he also instructs his young son on the warrior code. In a scene at once harsh and tender, epic and human, Aias appears not only as a shadow of his former self but also as the shadow of Hektor, the archenemy to whose fate his own is ironically linked. Now, more visibly than ever, through this shadow play of his enemy's fate, Aias appears little more than a memory, a "fleeting shadow" of that lost heroic world.

But Sophocles undercuts even this humanly revealing moment. The outmoded epic hero is finally too implacable to assume his new human role with grace. Displaced from his epic context, as in the opening scene, Aias appears absurdly ruthless; but, even in this Homeric farewell scene, he seems relatively grim. He has no such consoling words for Tekmessa as Hektor had for Andromache, whose day of slavery grieves him more than the deaths of all his family. Hektor's are strong words, but there is nothing like them in Sophocles' play: "She will win my praise / if she does what I command" (589 f.) is all that Aias says. Tekmessa's appeal does not persuade Aias to accept her tragic view — "My lord, there is no greater evil / among us than inescapable / chance (538–40) — although his own fate confirms her words. She who was once Aias' captive now loves him; the Greeks who were his friends now hate him. Odysseus whom he most hates pities him; and, "by chance," Aias the man "like none other" reenacts the fate of the enemy he fought so hard to destroy. In madness Aias was degraded. But even in his farewell to Tekmessa and his son he is hard and stubborn: "It is foolish," he says to Tekmessa in parting, "to think you can school me now!" (673 f.).

III

Aias has now made his exit, and the chorus sings: "Let Hades hide him, his affliction has gone / beyond all measure (702 f.) . . . Oh, luckless father, you've yet / to learn what unbearable end / your son has come to . . ." (707–9). The chorus confirms what has been anticipated: Aias has gone to die. At this point, the audience doubtless expects the great messenger speech of the play, like that perhaps of Aeschylus' vivid account of the hero's last moments: "like a man stretching a bow, he bent back the sword on his impenetrable skin" (frg. 83N).

Instead, expectations are disappointed. What follows is indeed the play's great speech. Not a messenger's speech *about* Aias, but a meditation on mutability delivered *by* Aias. The audience believes that Aias is in his tent, either dead already or dying. But Sophocles has surprisingly reshaped the myth so as to reveal now the emergence of the new Aias, whose speech and suicide will transform the meaning of his myth:

> Great, unfathomable time
> brings dark things into the light
> and buries the bright in darkness.
> Nothing is too strange, time seizes
> the most dread oath, the most hardened
> mind. Even I . . .
>
> (712–17)

The play has indeed brought a "dark thing to light": that mad, blood-stained Aias who inspired Odysseus' reflections on our tragically shadowy existence. Pindar had attributed the eclipse of Aias to human treachery: "Guile . . . drives splendor into darkness and honors the obscure." But Sophocles' Aias sees *beyond* his own tragedy into a universal darkness; there is a brutal mutability at the heart of things — betrayal, god-inflicted madness, and degradation are merely its symptoms. No Sophoclean play is so concerned with time and so saturated with temporal expressions ("always," first word of the play in Greek, "sometimes," "in time," "whenever," "never"). But Aias is the first to see clearly what the chorus will realize only later—much too late— when it sings, "Time, since the best men / contended for the arms of Achilles, / has been a potent begetter of sorrows" (1032 ff.). The world of Aias is a universe in flux, modeled perhaps on Heraclitus' river of change but without the philosopher's comforting hint of continuity. In this world only one thing is certain: uncertainty. From this law nothing is exempt, not "the most dread oath, the most hardened / mind." Not even Aias.

This speech is the heart of the play, the moment of fatal choice. Aias sees the world for what it is but, by deciding to move *against* the flow, *becomes* himself. Because Tekmessa and the chorus misunderstand Aias' resolve, the speech has been dubbed the "deception speech." Nothing could be further from the truth. Sophocles has not composed this speech, surely one of the greatest in Greek drama, so that the man of absolute honor may tell lies. In fact, Aias does not even speak to Tekmessa and the chorus. He enters, deep in thought, and delivers an unprecedented monologue-in-the-presence-of-others. This tragic isolation of the hero, even while surrounded by his friends, is profoundly Sophoclean. Aias no longer belongs to the world of others. He is involved in a final struggle with his own *daimon*, which, like its emblem the sword, now appears hostile and alien.

Here and only here Aias speaks with two voices. But these are not voices of uncertainty. Rather, we see two Aiases: one Aias who recognizes the law of change by which all else lives and dies; another Aias who will act in accord with the absolute law of his own nature. The speech is pure drama, in the sense that its meaning is inseparable from its dramatic context. As T. S. Eliot remarked of some of Shakespeare's great speeches:

> The lines are surprising, and yet they fit in with the character; or else we are compelled to *adjust our conception of the character in such a way that the lines will be appropriate to it* . . . dramatic . . . poetry . . . does not interrupt but intensifies the dramatic situation . . . you can hardly say whether the lines give grandeur to the drama, or whether it is the drama which turns the words into poetry.[3]

The Aias who *seems* to soften, who *seems* capable of living in a world of double meanings, is the *fondo* from which the new Aias, the fatal Aias, emerges. The drama lies in the agony with which the warrior-hero speaks, first words of pity, then words of reconciliation ("we will know / how to yield to the gods"[739 f.]), and finally in the scorn with which he describes submission ("bow down before the Atreidai" [741]). Aias uses the same word (*loutra*) of cleansing and purification ("I will go to a bathing place" [724]) that is later used to describe the ritual of his death (1597). His fate speaks *through* and *in* his *daimon*, even as his words appear to deny it.

At the outset Aias describes himself as "unbending / in action"

3. T.S. Eliot, "Poetry and Drama," *On Poetry and Poets* (Farrar, Straus & Giroux, 1975), p. 89 (originally published 1951); "Yeats," *idem.*, p. 305 (originally published 1940).

(718 f.). He now asserts his presence among "the most unbending" elemental powers, though they are, ironically, his models of submission:

> ... snow-tracked
> winter yields to the rich growth
> of summer, dark-vaulted night
> gives way to the shining, white-horsed
> brightness of day, a blast
> of appalling wind stills the sea's rage,
> even all-overwhelming sleep
> binds only to let go ...
>
> (744–51)

The succession in each case—winter to summer, night to day, storm to calm—is characterized by movement from "dark" to "light." The final term is sleep, but the antithesis—waking—is missing. The ellipsis will be answered by an action. "All-overwhelming sleep" epitomizes the world's condition, tossed to and fro in the oblivion of change. Yet, even as he speaks, Aias is on the threshold of "awaking" into another order, "a world elsewhere."

Moving purposively from the god-sent "storm" of darkness, Aias at last arrives at fatal clarity. He speaks with sarcasm ("Then how / shall we not learn wise restraint?" 751 f.), which betrays absolute certainty. In his closing reflection on the frailty of friendship and enmity alike, Aias tells what cosmic mutability means in human terms:

> I know now to hate an enemy
> just so far, so that another time
> we may befriend him. And the friend
> I help, I will not help too greatly,
> knowing that one day will find him
> my enemy.
>
> (753–58)

In a world where nothing lasts, where even the inexorable forces of nature change, little can be expected of fragile human feeling. The Aias who ends his speech with a *topos* on treachery ("For most mortals / friendship is a treacherous harbor," [758 f.]) has already decided that he will no longer live in *this* world—and still be Aias. He now *knows*: the absolute moment of his life is his death. To *go on* being Aias he must end his life—beyond choice, chance, change. At the close of the speech there is no further ambiguity. Aias *becomes* himself—by ceasing to be.

Something innately human has pushed Aias beyond contingency: love, the other side of his equally absolute hatred. His first intelligible word was a call for his son (370), followed by a cry for his brother (373), then an address to his "friends, / my only true-minded friends" (381 f.). Moreover, he has left specific instructions for the care of his old parents, that his son be brought to "ease the weight of their years" (642). And just before he dies, between his farewell to the light and invocation of death, Aias will think of his poor parents' grief. But what of his brusque way with Tekmessa? Surely he rebuffs her because he is vulnerable to her above all. Between them is a kindness (*charis*) greater than kinship. As the chorus said, Aias won her by the spear, but she won his heart (229 ff.). His harshness with her is a resistance to what she alone can do, what even time cannot do: change Aias "Even I, whose will / was tempered like iron, unbending / in action, for a woman's sake / am become a woman in my speech" (717 ff.). His seeming callousness conceals his real human vulnerability. Aias loves absolutely; and so to achieve permanence—the principle that preserves love itself—he must paradoxically leave those he loves. He will not accept a world in which the absolute values of love, friendship, oaths, honor, even hatred do not last. The words spoken by another unconditional lover, Shakespeare's Cleopatra, in the scene leading to her triumphant suicide, might have been those of Aias:

> . . . and it is great
> To do that thing that ends all other deeds;
> Which shackles accidents and bolts up change.
> (*Antony and Cleopatra* act 5, scene 2)

An overpowering human force drives Aias beyond the human, allowing him to transform death into destiny, without relinquishing his absolutes. Only an immutable act can defeat the enemy that undermines all "human things"—"great, unfathomable time." That Tekmessa and the chorus fail to understand his words only heightens the power of the speech and dramatizes the solitude in which the hero's fatal struggle with his *daimon* has taken place. "I will go," says Aias, "where I have to go" (767).

IV

The certainty of his final words, however, dissolves in the chorus's sudden ecstatic reaction to them. There was matter in the speech itself to induce hope and prepare the audience for a denial of the suicide convention. Song and dance, moreover, are strong medicine ("Desire thrills in me, joy gives me wings!" [770]), and an audience cannot remain wholly unaffected. Sophocles was famous for these odes of joyous delusion, but perhaps nowhere else are they used to such dramatic effect. We now *feel hope* as we *felt despair* in the preceding choral dirge. Suspense and song draw us into the choral world of change, possibility, and therefore hope. *"Time truly is great . . . / nothing's too strange /* if Aias can turn / his heart from hatred" (791 ff. [emphasis added]), the enrapt chorus sings, echoing Aias' words but reversing his meaning. The poet *dramatizes* the gulf separating us from Aias and his fatal certainty.

Even the messenger who at last arrives is, contrary to expectation, a harbinger of uncertainty. In place of the long-awaited account of the hero's death, we are told that Aias' life is contingent upon "this [one] day's light" (832)—the point is stressed four times—the length of Athene's anger. Aias has scorned those men whose lives are measured by days, "day after day / moving forward or back from the end line / of death" (525 ff.), and it is just this which Tekmessa and the chorus's to-ing and fro-ing, in the hope of saving Aias, now dramatizes. The messenger also presents still another distortion of the traditional image of Aias. Speaking the familiar language of Greek morality, the messenger describes Aias as a man of *hybris*—an "outsized body" untamed by human thoughts (838 ff.). His account of Aias' blasphemous words to Athene ("Go . . . stand by the rest of the Greeks. / The line won't break where I hold it" [857 ff.]) has no epic precedent and consorts strangely with Aias' words of gratitude for what he earlier thought was Athene's divine alliance.

But Aias has "let [his mind] go beyond the human" (840) and truly "owe[s] nothing more to the gods" (668), though not in the sense that such presumptuousness is usually understood. Aias has indeed passed so far beyond both the "human" and the messenger's "divine" that Sophocles feels it necessary to empty the stage—an extremely rare occurrence in extant drama—in order to prepare for Aias' appearance. We are suddenly in another world, a liminal space where the opposed realities of land and sea, heaven and earth, converge. The grave tableau—Aias beside his upright sword—is now rolled out on the *ekkyklema*. At last, the true nature of his defiance, that of the *metaphysically* stiff-necked man, will be revealed.

The "killer" sword stands ready, firmly planted by Aias. In Homer the sword symbolized certainty and honor; here it is the visual emblem of change, an image of Aias' fate, a present from Hektor, "an enemy's gift" (737) to the man who won only enmity from friends. Sharpened on the "iron-eating stone" (915), the sword is destiny for the rocklike man, "whose will / was tempered like iron, unbending / in action" (717 f.). But in the sword we also have an image of that force behind all flux, Aias' real enemy—Time. Imagine how this sword might have appeared to those sitting in the Theater of Dionysus: the blade straight up, in the early morning light, it must have cast a long shadow—like the needle of a giant sundial—across the *ekkyklema* on which Aias stands. It is "Time's sword," moving even as Aias speaks. The hero's character now requires that he enact the truth of his own words. As Time's sword moves "against" Aias, so he moves to make Time stop.

Zeus, Hermes, even Death are now, in Aias' words, made to wait on him. The gods he invokes are not, like Athene, powers of contingency who meddle with men. He invokes these gods solely as guardians of the dead, divinities of passage to man's "long home," beyond time, beyond change. Curses in the name of the primeval Furies assure his *eternal* hatred of the Greeks. But his most striking and significant address is to Helios, specifically as heavenly charioteer. Speaking in mythical terms, Aias commands Helios to rein in his chariot: to halt the Sun is to stop Time. Aias has transformed his death into an epiphany of permanence. His huge body covering the sword, he will eclipse Time and die, not in darkness, but, as his final invocation suggests, radiantly in the light. Now the unbending, immovable Aias has at last appeared. There is no trace of the lamenting Aias or the mad Aias of the opening scenes, or the shadowy "relenting" Aias of the Time speech; there is only the inflexible, commanding presence that here triumphs and destroys itself. We see his *ethos* become his *daimon*. He exceeds the world he is in, and passes beyond it. But in contrast to Homer's mute shade, this Aias promises speech in death: "I *will speak* to the dead in Hades" (965 [emphasis added]), or, as *mythēsomai*, his final word, declares, "live on as undying 'myth.'"

Aias has decided; and the "day" has been made to attend upon his decision. Even Odysseus' tragic wisdom about "fleeting shadows" has been refuted. Indeed, Aias' stature grows until he literally touches the divine. He demands and achieves something that is not of the temporal world. His final invocation of heavenly light and sustaining earth ("... O radiance! / O holy ground" [957 f.]) suggests something like the apotheosis of Oedipus at Colonus. The hero belongs to both heaven and earth. Elemental powers—divine *physis*, the eternality of Nature herself, not her changing seasons—are summoned from above and below to converge upon the hero. For Sophocles, men at the peak of their powers *reveal* the gods who are *there* but unrealized until men disclose them.

V

Does the suicide take place in view of the audience or not? The question is crucial, but unfortunately, our text provides no unequivocal answer. If, as Aias spoke his last words, he leapt on his sword, this would be the unique instance of dramatized violence in Greek tragedy. In any case, Sophocles is not concerned with a sensational suicide but rather with the *meaning* of the act. As with the Oedipus' self-blinding, it is the vision—it is the outward seeing transformed into inward sight—that matters, not the violence of the plunging blade. Aias finally had to move beyond words, to the enactment of his truth; at this point, verbal meaning becomes visual. And it is this that takes place in the coming scene with Teukros.

Teukros' arrival has been long awaited. Aias has three times referred to his coming (373 f., 631 ff., 764 ff.), and now Tekmessa anticipates it (884 f., 1018 ff.). The significance of his arrival is linked to the preceding events. As Aias finishes his speech, he and the sword are trundled inside the stage building. The chorus enter the orchestra in confusion, followed by Tekmessa beside the body of Aias on the *ekkyklema*. But the chorus do not in fact see Aias (1008 ff.). More important, their request to see him is emphatically refused by Tekmessa:

> He must not be seen! I will cover
> his body, I will wrap him completely
> in my mantle . . .
>
> (1010 ff.)

If the chorus cannot see the body, neither can the audience. The concealment suggests that later the body will be uncovered. But Tekmessa, who had urged Aias to accept contingency and who, like the chorus, is resigned to the tyranny of time, is not the proper person to uncover the body and reveal the heroic truth Aias has enacted.

The following scene is all revelation. The question "Where is Teukros?" is at last answered. The plot requires his coming in order to protect Aias' dependents, but his arrival is carefully linked to the concealing of the body (1010 ff.) His long speech begins with three sight words: ". . . of all my eyes have seen / this is the most painful sight" (1099 f.). The point could hardly be more emphatic. Teukros now asks for visible confirmation of what he has heard. "Uncover him," he finally says to Tekmessa, "let me look at the whole evil" (1109 f.).

The *face* of Aias is what he sees: "that hard face, / that grim self-command!" (1111 f.)—literally, "that face hard to see, full of bitter daring" (*o dystheaton omma kai tolmēs pikras*). The line makes it clear that Aias has fallen sideways on his sword, and that he now lies impaled *face-up*. His fierce face is a constant feature from Homer on; bright eyes and an eagle glare characterize him in the play (100 f., 189 ff.). This same grim face—staring up at radiant light—must be what Teukros is describing. Aias has faced death as he faced his enemies: head on, without fear. He is now revealed as a man who has dared to look at the world's truth and face its consequences rather than suffer its uncertainties. Anything but a "fleeting shadow," Aias dies at the height of his powers, a hero "in the light."

VI

The dead Aias dominates the stage more than ever, but the heated dispute over his burial now jeopardizes his *meaning*. A hero's burial had an aura of mystery quite alien to us. Like a canonized saint, the hero had the power to bless the land in which he was buried and the people who revered him. To deny Aias burial is not only to dishonor a great man and deny the "otherness" he embodies, but to violate the sacred laws that bind the living to the dead. When the hero refused burial is also an Athenian hero, the morality of the "sacred city" itself is at stake.

But the tangible dramatic difference of the second half of the play has led critics to complain that the play is clumsily composed. The hero is "gone" by midpoint, and the remainder of the play seems merely an extended debate. Plays such as *Antigone*, *Oedipus Rex*, or *Women of Trachis* close with a crescendo. The diminuendo here is undeniable. But the purpose is certainly to dramatize how the world would be without an Aias. The unheroic tone of the speeches with their threats, boasts, and insults reveal the meanness of this new world. Heroism seems to have died with Aias on his sword. The great speeches earlier, rich with noble epic language, are all spoken by Aias. The lyric mode itself, tragedy's "higher voice," fades away; the first half of the play contains four choral odes, the last half has only one. Grandeur of every kind diminished or vanished, the loss of Aias becomes achingly real. Absent, he is powerfully present in a world of smaller men. Even as a corpse, he dwarfs the survivors (good and bad alike). As the chorus sang in their entrance song, ". . . small men / crumble without the great" (181 f.).

When presented, the *Aias* reportedly aroused a violent reaction. We will never know what nerve the final five hundred lines of this play touched. But something in Athenian experience must surely be related to the passing of the heroic age that these last scenes dramatize. Tentatively dated to c. 445–40 B.C., the play would seem to have been produced at a time when Athens was examining the policies and perhaps the morality of her empire. Political arrogance resonates in the rhetoric and power politics of the very un-Homeric Agamemnon and Menelaos. But nothing is served by identifying the particular contemporary types represented by the Atreidai. They may be Spartan oligarchs or the amoral expansionists of imperial Athens. In any case, they are despots who possess political, not moral, authority and whose power rests upon fear and exploitation of others. Such men are found almost anywhere, at almost any time. Aias' greatness was based upon the *arete* implicit in Odysseus' description of him. But true greatness is rare, and the Atreidai's "principled" outrage is merely a perversion of Aias' heroic *hybris*. Aias' supreme self-assertion was of an altogether different order, anything but the basely selfish "morality" of the Atreidai.

Which leaves Odysseus as Aias' improbable moral heir. The compassionate and conciliatory Odysseus of the last scene (the only favorable portrayal of him in extant tragedy) represents the new ethos of democratic Athens at its best. In his speech on Time, Aias predicted that harshness would yield to gentleness. *Aristos* — the term earlier applied to Aias — is now applied to Odysseus by Teukros. Like Aias, Odysseus also honors friendship, recognizing that the *arete* of the dead Aias trivializes their former enmity: "I am moved more by his greatness / than by my enmity" (1537 f.).

Odysseus' final exchange with Agamemnon paradoxically engages the terms *friend* and *enemy*. For Odysseus, they are relative terms: a confirmation of the contingent morality resolutely rejected by Aias. But, though canny and adaptive, Odysseus is no moral opportunist. He speaks as a man who understands that since all men suffer the same fate, compassion and compromise are the appropriate virtues. And he is therefore able to adapt even the self-willed exceptional man, Aias, to his democratic vision. As in the earlier scene, the sight of Aias inspires Odysseus' tragic view of humanity. His earlier reflection of human transience is a tragic *topos*, poetically expressed ("phantoms, fleeting shadows"); his advice to Agamemnon arises from this same vision but is put very differently. Now Odysseus' words suggest a practical strategy with political implications — a basis, in other words, for human (and Athenian) democracy:

AGAMEMNON I must let them bury the body,
is that what you say?

ODYSSEUS It is.
I will face the same need some day.

AGAMEMNON It is all one, then, and each man works
for himself.

> ODYSSEUS There is reason in that.
> Who else should I work for?
>
> (1547–52)

This is not Homeric individualism in the grand manner; but neither is it the opportunistic selfishness of the final years of the Athenian fifth century. It is both political and tragic wisdom: the foundation for a society in which compassion is perceived as the basis of preservation. Thucydides wrote:

> ... men too often take upon themselves in the prosecution of their revenge to set the example of doing away with those general laws to which all alike can look for salvation in adversity, instead of allowing them to subsist against the day of danger when their aid may be required.
>
> (3.84, Crawley transl.)

Odysseus, contrary to expectation, shows how society might preserve not only "that ancient simplicity into which honor so largely entered" (3.83) but also those endangered "general laws."

But Sophocles refuses full closure. The audience instead is challenged by a paradox. Despite his mediating role, Odysseus is not allowed to touch the hero's body; Aias, even dead, is resolute in his hatred. If that huge body commanding the stage is seen as inimical to Odysseus, then how can the spirit that animated it ever be domiciled in Athens? In the single choral ode after Aias' death, an ode beginning in despair but ending in hope (1331–66), the chorus strives for a resolution. How long, they ask, will the Trojan War last, and they recall happier times, days of wine, song, sleep, and love-making. These sentiments of ordinary life, seemingly anomalous in high tragedy, compel us to ask what impulse lies behind them? Surely, what the chorus sees—the tableau of Aias protected by his loved ones that dominates the play at its close.

Tekmessa and Eurysakes kneel over the body. The boy holds three locks of hair, with which he supplicates his dead father. Mother, son, and father form a tableau of *philia*, the "human bond" by which the dead and the living are joined in sacrament. Moved by the spectacle, the chorus remember *their* "world elsewhere," that of their loved ones, the joy and peace they have left behind them. They then lament the loss of the man on whom their return depended, their "great wall / against weapons and terrors / under the pall of night . . . relentless Aias" (1355 ff.). What joy is left, the chorus asks, now that their Aias is dead

(1361 f.)? They conclude, however, by expressing their yearning to sail toward the "wooded rampart of Sounion" and "holy Athens" (1363, 1366). What they might have hoped for while Aias lived—the pleasures of peace and home—now lies in Athens, the city so renowned for its compassion toward exiles and suppliants.

The point is made and confirmed by the poet's fusion of hero and city in the double image of a "bulwark": "relentless" Aias, "the great wall" (*probola* [1355]) and the "rampart" (*problēma* 1363 f.) of Sounion, the promontory where Attica most vividly meets the sea. Epic bulwark and Attic headland merge into what even the Theban Pindar had hailed as the "bulwark of Greece, holy Athens" (frg. 76). In the final scene, by applying to Odysseus the epithet *aristos*, elsewhere reserved for Aias, Teukros signals the emergence of a new *arete*, different from that of Aias, but originating nonetheless in his myth. By reconciling others to Aias, Odysseus demonstrates that the hero—daimonic even in hatred—is an enduring "presence," a power indispensable to that city that claimed to be "the education of Hellas." Just as the city needs the hero, so the hero, at least in death, needs others, needs the city and the human solidarity it represents. But now the burden of heroism must belong to all; aristocratic *arete* must be democratized. But ultimately the chorus's new "bulwark" preserves the image of unyielding Aias—Homer's "wave-beaten ridge," that Sophoclean "rock in the sea" which, like old Oedipus, "abides the coming of the waves." For the "divine" in "human things," for the values of endurance, tragic solitude, and heroic hybris—the basis of the permanent values that energize the democratic city—Aias is the paradigm.

And so the play rightly closes with Aias. The final image is an image of blood—not animal blood as in the first scene, but the human blood of Aias. Body, burial, a hero's blood—these are now the final revealing images. Teukros, Eurysakes, and the chorus lift Aias whose "black life force . . . still flowing out / of his warm veins" (1601 f.) now covers those who hold him. Blood-violence has become blood-bond, the link that binds living and dead, city and hero, "radiance" and "holy ground."

Boston, Mass.   HERBERT GOLDER
1998

ON THE TRANSLATION

The dialogues in this version of the *Aías* are composed in sprung rhythm, with three stresses to a line. There is no set pattern in which the stresses fall and no rule governing the number of unstressed syllables in the line. The stresses may be single or doubled. This system allows for lines as brief as

I will bury Alas

or as long as

There were swords drawn. It would have gone badly

to be read as prosodically equivalent. Sprung rhythm is the natural rhythm of speech heightened by the formal constraint of a fixed number of stresses and the ear's perception of regularity behind the irregularity. Keeping the number of stresses in mind will also help the reader (or actor) to hear how the lines should be spoken.

The choral odes and other more formal passages in the play (162–279 for instance) are also in sprung rhythm, with lines of one to five stresses. They mirror the structures of the original. The entrance of the chorus (*parados*, 162–191) is composed in a rocking four-stress line, as is the final *exodus* (1594–1608), with its brief anticipation in lines 1304–8.

I hope that these poetic principles have enabled us to avoid the effect of the double iambic trimeter, the meter of dialogue in Greek drama ("I see you've come on foot, not riding on a horse"), which can be rather ludicrous in English, and at the same time to make an actable version of the play that keeps some sense of the high formality of Greek tragedy, so often lost in free-verse translations.

Mention should be made of our use of certain Greek outcries and lamenting words: *Io! Io moi moi! Omoi! Aiai!* English has almost no such words, yet to eliminate them from the *Aias* seemed a grave loss. Instead, we have followed the example of Paul Claudel, whose great French translation of the *Agamemnon* allows for such cries as: *Otototoï! Iô popoï! Iou iou!* and *oïmoï!* The reader will understand that these are not so much words as noises. King Lear makes his last entrance with the line: "Howl, howl, howl, howl! O, you are men of stones!" And so I always read it. Only when I saw the play performed did I realize that the old man enters *howling*.

RICHARD PEVEAR

AIAS

CHARACTERS

ATHENE

ODYSSEUS

AIAS

CHORUS of Sailors from Salamis

TEKMESSA wife of Aias

EURYSAKES son of Aias

MESSENGER

ATTENDANTS of Aias

TEUKROS half-brother of Aias

MENELAOS

ARMED ATTENDANTS of the Atreidai

AGAMEMNON

Line numbers in the right-hand margin of the text refer to the English translation only, and the Notes on the text at p. 81 are keyed to these lines. The bracketed line numbers in the running head lines refer to the Greek text.

The scene is the Greek camp on the coast at Troy. The stage building represents the
quarters of AIAS *surrounded by a stockade with double gates in the center.*

ATHENE *appears aloft.*

ODYSSEUS *enters from the side.*

ATHENE   I always see you like this,
　　　　　Odysseus, hunting out some advantage
　　　　　against your enemies. Now
　　　　　you're sniffing around where Aias
　　　　　and his sailors pitched their tents
　　　　　at the end of the battle line,
　　　　　pacing over his fresh tracks, wondering
　　　　　if he has gone in or is still
　　　　　out roaming. The scent has led you
　　　　　like a sharp-nosed Spartan bitch　　　　　　　　　　10
　　　　　to the right place. No need
　　　　　to peer through the gates: he's there,
　　　　　his head and sword-slaying hands
　　　　　still dripping sweat. But tell me,
　　　　　why are you pursuing him?
　　　　　You may learn from what I know.

ODYSSEUS   Athene! No god is closer
　　　　　to my heart! I cannot see you
　　　　　but your words ring like a bronze-mouthed
　　　　　trumpet in my mind. You're right,　　　　　　　　20
　　　　　I'm hunting an enemy, circling
　　　　　his footprints: Aias, the great shield.
　　　　　Last night he did something in-
　　　　　conceivable—or he may have done it,
　　　　　nothing's sure, we're still bewildered.
　　　　　I took the burden of proof
　　　　　on myself. Just now we found
　　　　　all our spoil of cattle,
　　　　　herds and herdsmen, butchered,
　　　　　torn to pieces by some monstrous　　　　　　　　30

27

hand—his hand, we think.
A witness claims he saw him
leaping across the field
alone, swinging a wet sword.
When I heard that, I sought out
the trail, and it led me here.
But these tracks baffle me: some
I know are his, but the others
are hard to make out. You've come
when I most needed you, goddess!   40
Your hand has always steered me
and always will.

ATHENE   I knew that.
I've been following you for some time,
caught up in the hunt myself.

ODYSSEUS Then my tracking has not gone wrong?

ATHENE I assure you, the man did everything
you have said.

ODYSSEUS   A reckless hand!
What drove him to it?

ATHENE   Rage
over the award of Achilles' armor.

ODYSSEUS But why slaughter the cattle?   50

ATHENE He thought he was smearing his hands
with your blood.

ODYSSEUS   With ours?
Then he meant to kill Greeks?

ATHENE   And would have
if I had not been watching.

ODYSSEUS What nerved him, what made him dare?

ATHENE He came stalking you in the darkness.

ODYSSEUS Was he close? Could he have struck?

ATHENE He was at the two generals' gates.

ODYSSEUS And so eager to kill—what stopped him?

ATHENE I stopped him. Spinning illusions   60
of his own most deadly joy,
I drew him to your captured herds
milling in the field. He fell on them,
hacking at sheep and cattle,
crushing their spines, carving out
a bloody circle around him.
Sometimes he thought the Atreidai
were in his huge grip, then he struck
at another chief and another,
roving up and down in a sick frenzy.   70
And I urged him on, I drove him
deeper into the net.
At last he grew tired of killing,
bound up what cattle and sheep
were left alive and dragged them
to his camp—all horns and hoofs,
but he thinks they're men. He has them
inside there now. He's torturing them.
      But I want you to see this sickness
with your own eyes and proclaim it   80
aloud to all the Greeks.

                    ODYSSEUS *averts his eyes and turns to leave.*

Stay! Face him! What he has become
is no threat to you. I'll bend
the light of his eyes away.
He won't see you standing there.
                              Aias!
Leave off chaining your captives
and come out here!

ODYSSEUS   Athene!
          Do not call him out!

ATHENE   Quiet!
          Or shall men say you're a coward?

ODYSSEUS By the gods, no! But leave him inside.   90

ATHENE Why? Isn't he the same man he was?

ODYSSEUS The same, yes, and still my enemy.

ATHENE And is any laughter sweeter
          than laughter at an enemy?

ODYSSEUS Even so, let him stay inside.

ATHENE Are you afraid to look in the eyes
          of a madman?

ODYSSEUS   If he were not mad
          I would face him.

ATHENE   Face him now, then.
          Even this close, he won't see you.

ODYSSEUS How not, if he has the same eyes?   100

ATHENE Bright as they are, I'll darken them.

ODYSSEUS Gods can contrive what they please.

ATHENE Stand there and say nothing.

ODYSSEUS If I must, I will, but I would sooner
          be far from this place.

ATHENE   Aias!
          I call you again. Does your ally
          count for so little now?

A blood-smeared AIAS *enters through central gates. His*
speeches are interspersed with savage laughter.

AIAS   Hail to you, Athene, hail to you,
        daughter of Zeus! Ah, how well
        you stood by me in this night's work!   110
        I'll crown you with gold for it!

ATHENE Beautiful words. But tell me,
        did your sword drink deeply of Greek blood?

AIAS   I boast it did. Why deny it?

ATHENE Did your spear find the Atreidai?

AIAS   Aias will not be dishonored
        by those two again.

ATHENE   They're dead,
        if I understand you?

AIAS   Dead!
        Let them rob me of the armor now!

ATHENE And what of the son of Laertes?   120
        Where does he stand between you
        and his ill fate? Has he escaped you?

AIAS   That slinking weasel—you ask me
        where he is now?

ATHENE   Yes,
        that great obstacle of yours—Odysseus.

AIAS   My sweetest triumph, goddess.
        He's cowering inside there, in chains.
        I don't want him to die yet.

ATHENE What more would you have first?

AIAS   First tie him to a post in the yard.   130

31

ATHENE The poor wretch. What will you do then?

AIAS Then flay his back with this whip
before I kill him.

ATHENE   Ah!
Poor wretch, must he suffer so?

AIAS Be content to have your way
in all else, Athene. The man
will pay that price and no other.

ATHENE As you please, then. Let your hand
know the joys your mind is bent on.

AIAS I go back to my work. And you, goddess,   140
I charge you, always stand by me
as you did in this past night.

AIAS *exits through the gates, which close behind him.*

ATHENE You see how strong the gods are,
Odysseus. Was there ever a man
of greater foresight than Aias
or prompter in the shifts of action?

ODYSSEUS None that I know. Yet I pity
the poor wretch, though he's my enemy.
He's yoked to an evil delusion,
but the same fate could be mine.   150
I see clearly: we who live
are all phantoms, fleeting shadows.

ATHENE Consider him well, then, and never
allow yourself to speak arrogant
words against the gods,
or feel proud if your hand strikes harder
than another's or wealth heaps higher
around you. One day can lift up
and bring down all human things.
The gods favor wise restraint   160
in men and hate transgressors.

ATHENE *disappears,* ODYSSEUS *exits. The* CHORUS *enters
marching in rhythm with their words.*

CHORUS   *parodos*

Son of Telamon, holder of power
on deep anchored, sea-ringed Salamis,
    when you do well I rejoice.
But to see you struck by Zeus, to hear
the Greeks cry slander against you, I tremble,
    dove-eyed terror comes over me.
Now from the fading night a loud murmur
has risen, disgracing us, saying you broke
across the horse-maddening meadows, killing   170
sheep and cattle, the plunder of allied
    spears in a blaze of iron.
Odysseus, persuasive Odysseus, shaped
these whispering words and finds ears eager
to hear them among your rivals, and each one
takes more pleasure in the tale, cursing
    your pain with outrageous laughter.
A great soul makes an easy target.
The same things said against me would miss.
Envy dogs the man of power.   180
Yet as a wall of defense small men
crumble without the great; when a great man
leads them, they rise and hold him higher.
    Fools will learn that the hard way.
Now they are shouting you down, and we have
no strength to turn away their attacks
without you, lord. Safe from your eye,
they chatter like a restless flock of starlings.
But show yourself, let a great eagle suddenly
tower above them, you'll see them huddle   190
    terror-struck, speechless with fear.

(The entrance chant turns to lyric invocation.)

Artemis of the bull cult, daughter   *strophe*
of Zeus—O terrible rumor, O
    mother of my disgrace—was it
she who drove you against the Greek herds
because of some victory left unpaid-for?

Was it shining battle spoil
she was cheated of, or gifts of the deer hunt?
Did bronze-chested Ares or Enyalios
curse the work of your spear, spinning   200
a night plot to avenge the outrage?

Your own mind, son of Telamon,   *antistrophe*
would not have led you so far wrong
to war against sheep and cattle.
It must be some sickness sent by the gods.
Zeus, Apollo, save us from slander!
If they are spreading lies,
if the great kings or that son of the vile
race of Sisyphos whisper evil,
O lord, do not sit in your tent by the sea   210
and let their malice go unopposed.

Up from your seat!   *epode*
You've been stuck fast
too long in this embattled silence.
Ruin fires heaven!
Enemy arrogance is fanned to flame
by a high wind in the wooded valleys.
While they all fleer
with cutting tongues,
my grief cannot move.   220

TEKMESSA *enters through the gates.*

TEKMESSA Friends who serve on the ship of Aias,
sons of the earth-born race of Erechtheus,
we who care for the distant house
of Telamon must cry out, cry out now!
Our awesome, great, relentless hero
Aias has fallen
afflicted by a darkening storm.

CHORUS What burden has the night exchanged for the day's?
Daughter of Phrygian Teleutas,
hard-driving Aias won you for his bed   230
in war, but you have won his affection.
Tell us if you know what happened.

34

TEKMESSA How can I say the unspeakable? You
will hear about a suffering bitter
as death: madness struck him in the night,
his fame is defiled. There are such horrible
things in his tent, sacrificial victims
soaked in their own blood, oracles all
    too revealing of the hand that killed them.

CHORUS   *strophe*

                    What you say   240
            of that fiery man is the same
            unbearable, inescapable
rumor the Greek commanders have spread,
            and their telling makes it greater.
                Oh, I'm afraid
                of what will come now—
                his death shines in it.
                His frenzied hand
                and dark sword cut down
                the herds and herdsmen.   250

TEKMESSA Oh, that's it, that is where he came from!
The beasts were tied up, he dragged them inside,
threw them to the ground and cut their throats
    or tore them apart barehanded.
Then he seized on two quick-footed rams,
slashed out the tongue of one, cuts its head off
and threw the carcass aside; the other
    he bound to a stake and lashed
with a heavy leather harness, a hissing
two-thonged whip, reviling it in words   260
so inhuman, so full of evil, a daimon
    must have spoken through him.

CHORUS   *antistrophe*

                Time to cover
            our heads and slip away
                on foot somehow,
or board ship, bend our backs to the oars,
            and go wherever she wills.
                The double-ruling

35

                    Atreidai churn up
                    such threats, I fear   270
                    stones raining death
                    on him and us, held
                    by one awesome doom.

TEKMESSA But it's over now. The way flashing lightning
          dies with a gust of the south wind, he's come
          back to his senses. And found fresh pain.
          When a man looks at his own grief and knows
          that no one else was the cause of it, how much
              deeper the suffering cuts!

CHORUS But fortunately it is over.   280
        Evil means less once it's passed.

TEKMESSA Which would you choose if you could:
          pleasure for yourself despite
          your friends, or a share in their grief?

CHORUS Two griefs are worse, woman.

TEKMESSA Then his recovery is our ruin.

CHORUS I don't see what you mean.

TEKMESSA Those evils trapped him, but he
          took great pleasure in them
          because of his madness. For us   290
          they were agony. Then the madness
          passed, he caught his breath,
          and now he's hounded, driven
          to the limits of pain as we are.
          Is that not twice the evil?

CHORUS You're right. I'm afraid some god
        has struck him. It must be so
        if his pain grows worse as the sickness
        passes.

TEKMESSA   Strange, yet it's true.

CHORUS   But tell us, how did this evil   300
         come swooping down on him?
         We, too, suffer the harm of it.

TEKMESSA Since you are sharers, I'll tell you
         all I know. Long past midnight,
         when the torches were dead, he took
         his two-edged sword and groped
         his way to the door and the empty
         paths outside. I objected:
         "Aias, no one has called you,
         no messengers have come, no trumpets   310
         have sounded, the army's asleep.
         What are you doing?" His answer
         was brief, the much-sung refrain:
         "Silence becomes a woman,
         woman." So I let him teach me.
         He rushed out alone.

                              What happened
         then I can't say, but he came back
         dragging bulls, sheep dogs, sheep,
         all tied together. He took some
         and broke their necks, threw others   320
         on their backs and slaughtered them, cutting
         to the bone. A few he bound
         and tortured as if they were human.
         At one point he ran outside
         and spoke with some shadow, dredging up
         words against the Atreidai
         and Odysseus, mixed with laughter
         as violent as the revenge
         he claimed he had taken. Then he rushed
         back in where I was, and there   330
         slowly, painfully, in time,
         came to his senses. He looked
         at the place and all the carnage
         around him, beat his head
         and howled, and fell blood-smeared
         among the broken bodies, clawing
         at his face and hair.

                              He lay
         for a long time without speaking.

Then he turned to me and threatened me
with terrible words if I wouldn't   340
explain what had happened, asking me
where he stood now. Oh, my friends,
I was frightened, I told him everything
just as I'd seen it. And he wailed,
he wailed in anguish. Never
have I heard such sounds from him.
He used to say wailing was fit
for cowards and the heavy-hearted.
When he groaned it was no shrill
lament but deep like the bellow   350
of a bull.
            Now the man lies sprawled
in the wreck of his fate, surrounded
by the herds his iron brought down,
strangely calm, refusing to eat
or drink. It's clear he intends
to do some dreadful thing.
It sounds in his words and laments.
My friends, that's why I came out to you.
Go in, see if you can stop him.
Friends may win their friends back.   360

CHORUS   Tekmessa, daughter of Teleutas,
         by your words, the man's misfortunes
         have brought him to a dread extreme
         of possession.

AIAS   Io moi moi!

TEKMESSA There is worse to come, it seems.
          Did you hear that distorted howl?
          That was Aias!

AIAS   Io moi moi!

CHORUS   He's still mad, or sick from seeing
         what he did in his madness.

AIAS Io! Boy! My boy!   370

TEKMESSA Boy? Eurysakes! He wants you!
Oh, god, what for? Where are you?

AIAS Teukros! Where is Teukros! Forever
out raiding while I die here?

CHORUS The man seems to be in his senses.
Open the gates. If he sees us,
shame may bring him back.

TEKMESSA They are open. Now you can see
how he is and what he has done.

> TEKMESSA *opens the gates and* AIAS *is wheeled forward on*
> *a raised platform. He is sprawled among the carnage, and*
> *remains so as he addresses the* CHORUS *in song.*

AIAS   *strophe*
                        Io!   380
            Shipmates, friends,
            my only true-minded friends,
                look at me, look
                at the storm-driven wave
                of blood that has swamped me!

CHORUS You were right, too right! See
how far the madness drove him!

AIAS   *antistrophe*
                        Io!
            My men, skilled oarsmen,
            who ply the sea with your blades,   390
                you, you alone
                can end this suffering.
                Join now to kill me!

CHORUS No! Never say it, Aias!
If you try to cure evil with evil
you will add more pain to your fate.

AIAS   *strophe*

These hands that broke men,
that drove back armies, brought down
their terror on cattle! Oh,
the laughter! the outrage I've suffered!   400

TEKMESSA My lord, do not say these things!

AIAS Are you still here, woman?
Can you find no other pasture?
aiai! aiai!

TEKMESSA Give way, by the gods, relent!

AIAS

My hard fate to let
those devils slip through
my hands, to fall
on horned bulls and bright flocks
spilling their dark blood!   410

CHORUS What's done is done, reliving
the harm will not undo it.

AIAS   *antistrophe*

Spying everywhere, tool
of all evils, filthiest scum
of the army, Odysseus, you must be
somewhere laughing and gloating now!

CHORUS The gods say who laughs or cries.

AIAS Only let me set eyes on him . . . !
Io moi moi!

CHORUS Your words are too big, you forget   420
how deep in trouble you are.

AIAS

O Zeus, father
of my fathers, let me
kill that skulking
schemer and the two
high kings, and die!

TEKMESSA Pray for my death, too, then.
        What good is my life with you dead?

        AIAS   *strophe*
                        Io!
                Darkness, my light!   430
        brightest gloom, take me, take me
                to you, take me down into
                your house, I am not worthy
                    anymore to look
        for good from eternal gods or men of a day.
                    Zeus' daughter,
                the armored goddess,
            tortures me to death!
                Where can I escape?
                What place will keep me?   440
                My honor is dead,
        my friends, as dead as these creatures.
        I've been caught by my own fool's prey,
        and the whole army would gladly
                kill me twice over!

TEKMESSA It is hard to hear a great man
        say words he would once have despised.

        AIAS   *antistrophe*
                        Io!
                Sea-roaring straits,
        sea caves, groves, salt meadows   450
            by the shore, you've held me
            a long time at Troy, but
                no longer, no longer,
        not with breath in me, I promise you that!
                Skamander, river
                hostile to the Greeks,
            there is one man your water
                will not mirror
                again — I will have
                my full say — a man   460

like none Troy ever set eyes on
in all the armed host coming over
from Greece. But now I lie here
in filth and dishonor!

CHORUS I do not know how to stop you
or how I can let you go on,
seeing the evils you're caught in.

AIAS *rises slowly to his feet as the*
CHORUS *finishes speaking.*

AIAS Aiai! My name is a lament!
Who would have thought it would fit
so well with my misfortunes!   470
Now truly I can cry out—aiai!—
two and three times in my agony.
For I am a man whose father,
when he made war on this land,
came home with the greatest fame
and with the most beautiful spoils,
while I, that same man's son,
who brought as much strength to Troy,
whose acts were no less than his,
have won disgrace from the Greeks   480
and utter extinction!
                           Yet I know
one thing: if Achilles himself
had declared which man among us
was worthiest to bear his arms,
no one else would have touched them.
But the Atreidai seized the prize
instead, and gave it away
to a schemer, a man of all minds.
They scorned my mastery! I tell you,
if my eyes and mind had not   490
been wrenched wide of their mark,
those two with their ballots and voting
would turn no matter of justice
against anyone again! But the grim-eyed,
unbending daughter of Zeus
caught me as I brought my right hand

down on them, and drove me to madness.
I bloodied my hands on cattle.
They escaped, through no fault of mine,
and now they exult in their triumph,   500
laughing at me. With the help
of a god's tricks, any coward
can escape his betters.
                                        What now?
The gods hate me, that much is clear.
The Greek army detests me.
All Troy and the wide Trojan plain
are hostile to me. Shall I quit
this harbor, sail home across
the Aegean, and leave the Atreidai
to themselves? But what face can I show   510
my father Telamon? Could he bear
to see me come back stripped
of the high marks of honor that he
won here himself? Never.
Shall I go up to the walls of Troy
alone, take the army on, one
against all, show what I can do,
and die there? But that would only
please the Atreidai.
                                        No,
I must find some act that will prove   520
my nature and show my father
that his son was not born gutless.
To stretch your life out when you see
that nothing can break its misery
is shameful—day after day
moving forward or back from the end line
of death. There's no joy in that.
Any mortal who warms his heart
over empty hopes is worthless
in my eyes. Honor in life   530
or in death: if a man is born noble,
he must have one or the other.
You've heard all there is to say.

CHORUS   No one will claim these words
         are false to your birth or your heart,

Aias. But let them go now,
give your friends some part in your purpose.

TEKMESSA My lord, there is no greater evil
among us than inescapable
chance. My father was a free man,   540
as rich and powerful as any
in Phrygia. Now I am a slave.
I owe that to the gods, it seems,
and to your strength most of all.
Since the day I came to your bed
I have always done you honor.
Now I beg you by Zeus of the hearth
and by that bed which binds me to you,
do not think so little of me
as to leave me exposed to the scorn   550
of your enemies or the will of their hands.
If you die and abandon me,
know I'll be taken that same day
and dragged off with your son
to eat slave's food. And the Greeks,
my masters, will throw bitter words
in my face: "Do you see that woman?
Once she was concubine to Aias,
the strongest man in the army—
an enviable life. Now servitude   560
is all her reward!" They'll say more
and worse. The pain of that fate
will strike me, but the shame
of their words will strike you and all
your race.
                    Revere your father,
left alone in the misery of old age,
and your mother, with her portion of years,
who so often prays to the gods
that you will come home alive.
Pity your son, my lord,   570
facing his youth robbed of you,
in the keeping of indifferent strangers.
If you die, these are the evils
you will leave us to. There is nowhere
I can turn but to you. My homeland

vanished under your spear.
Fate took my mother and father down
to the dead in Hades. What other
home or wealth do I have?
You are my life. But remember,   580
my lord, what I've been for you.
If a man has known some pleasure,
he ought to be mindful of it.
Kindness begets kindness.
A man who takes his pleasure
and forgets it, cannot be noble.

CHORUS If your mind can be moved to pity
as mine is, Aias, you will praise
her words.

AIAS   She will win my praise
if she does what I command.   590

TEKMESSA I will always obey you, Aias.

AIAS Bring my son here, let me see him.

TEKMESSA Of course. It was only from fear
that I sent him away.

AIAS   Fear of this?

He points to himself and the gory spectacle.

Or of what else?

TEKMESSA   Fear that he might
cross paths with you and die.

AIAS Yes, that would suit my fate.

TEKMESSA I was guarding against that.

AIAS You did well. I praise your foresight.

TEKMESSA Then how may I serve you now?   600

AIAS Let me see my son's face. I would speak with him.

TEKMESSA Very well. He is close by.
        The attendants are watching over him.

AIAS Then why is he not here yet?

TEKMESSA Eurysakes, your father wants you.
        Take his hand and bring him here.

AIAS Are they crawling? Do they refuse
      to obey you?

TEKMESSA   They're coming now.

They approach AIAS.

AIAS Lift him up to me. The sight
      of fresh blood will not frighten him   610
      if he's truly my son. The colt
      must be broken early to his father's
      rough ways, and so be made like him
      in nature.

The boy is lifted into AIAS' *hands.*

              My son, I pray
      that chance will prove kinder to you
      than she was to me. If you match me
      in all else, you will not do badly.
            Oh, I could envy you even now,
      because you cannot see the evil
      in these things. Life is sweetest   620
      when we know nothing. But a day will come
      when you learn about joy and grief.
      Then show your father's enemies
      what sort of man you are
      and what sort he was who bred you.
      For now, feed on soft breezes,
      let your young soul play, and be
      a joy for your mother.

The Greeks
will not dare to harm or insult you
even without me, I know that.
Teukros will guard your gates
and raise you—a man unstinting
in his care, though now the hunt
for his enemies keeps him away.
You who manned my ships
and shared my battles, must share
that kindly service with him.
And give this command to Teukros:
he must take the boy home and present him
to Telamon and to my mother
Eriboia. His youth will forever
ease the weight of their years,
until they go down to the deep god.
And my arms must not be set up
by arbiters as a prize
in any warlike contest.
They must not fall to the Greeks,
not to the man who disgraced me!
You were named for this shield, Eurysakes—
sevenfold unpierceable oxhide.
Hold it by the thick braided grip
like this. The rest of the arms
will be buried with me.

*In a slow, almost ceremonial fashion, AIAS places
his small son's hand on the huge grip*

Quick now,
take him in and lock the gates.
This is no place for tears, woman.
How you all love to weep! Go inside.
A skillful doctor does not
moan prayers when a sore needs cutting.

CHORUS I don't like this sudden hurry.
Your words have too sharp an edge.

TEKMESSA Aias, my lord!
Say what your heart intends!

47

AIAS Stop questioning and prying!
      Wise restraint is best.

TEKMESSA I beg you in the name of your son
          and the gods, do not betray us!

AIAS You vex me! Can you not see
      I owe nothing more to the gods?

TEKMESSA That is impious!

AIAS   Save your words.

TEKMESSA Can't I move you?

AIAS   No more of that!   670

TEKMESSA I'm frightened, my lord!

AIAS   Shut the gates!

TEKMESSA For god's sake, soften!

AIAS   It is foolish
      to think you can school me now!

              TEKMESSA, EURYSAKES, *and* ATTENDANTS *exit through the*
              gates, followed by AIAS *as the platform is rolled back.*

CHORUS   *first stasimon*
                  Famous Salamis, you   *strophe*
          must still be there, wave-beaten, fortunate,
                  bright in the sea forever.
          My misery is being gone from you
          these long years under Ida, wasting
                  away month after month,
                  camped in the grassy fields,   680
                  knowing I may win only
          to an end in unseen, unfaceable Hades.

Now Aias, too, is my care   *antistrophe*
taken over, omoi, beyond all cure
by a god's madness, the man
you sent to win fame in the fury of Ares.
He brings grief to his friends, feeding
    his secret thoughts alone,
        and the honor due his great
        past deeds has fallen, fallen   690
friendless between the hate-filled Atreidai.

I can see his mother, grown with time   *strophe*
to white old age, on the day she hears
        how madness ravaged his mind —
            ailinon! ailinon!
There will be no nightingale's soft lament
    from her, ill-fated woman,
    but a sharp, keening cry
    drawn from deep inside,
    hands beating her breast   700
again and again and tearing her gray hair.

Let Hades hide him, his affliction has gone   *antistrophe*
beyond all measure, son of a great race,
        best of the battle-worn Greeks.
        His nature no longer
true-bred in anger, he wars with himself.
    Oh, luckless father, you've yet
    to learn what unbearable end
    your son has come to, the first
    of all the Aiakidai   710
to find fate set hard against him.

                    AIAS *enters through the gates, followed
                    by* TEKMESSA *and* EURYSAKES.

AIAS Great, unfathomable time
    brings dark things into the light
    and buries the bright in darkness.
    Nothing is too strange, time seizes
    the most dread oath, the most hardened
    mind. Even I, whose will

was tempered like iron, unbending
in action, for a woman's sake
am become a woman in my speech.   720
Yes, the thought of leaving her a widow,
surrounded by enemies, and my son
an orphan, moves me to pity.
   But I will go to a bathing place
and the salt meadows to be cleansed
of this filth, and I may still escape
the weight of the goddess's anger.
And finding some trackless place,
I will dig up the earth and bury
this sword of mine, the most hostile   730
of weapons, where no one will find it.
Let night and Hades keep it
safe from all eyes, for I swear
since the day I took it in gift
from Hektor, my greatest enemy,
I have had no love from the Greeks.
It is true, then: an enemy's gift
is no gift but a bringer of loss.
   And in time to come we will know
how to yield to the gods and learn   740
to bow down before the Atreidai.
They command and we must obey.
For even the most awesome powers
submit to authority: snow-tracked
winter yields to the rich growth
of summer, dark-vaulted night
gives way to the shining, white-horsed
brightness of day, a blast
of appalling wind stills the sea's rage,
even all-overwhelming sleep   750
binds only to let go. Then how
shall we not learn wise restraint?
   I know now to hate an enemy
just so far, for another time
we may befriend him. And the friend
I help, I will not help too greatly,
knowing that one day may find him
my enemy. For most mortals
friendship is a treacherous harbor.

But these things will all turn out well.
You, woman, go and pray to the gods
that my heart may see its desires
carried through to the end. Pray with her,
my friends. And when Teukros comes,
tell him these are my orders:
to look after us and treat you kindly.
I will go where I have to go.
Do as I've said. Fate is hard now,
but you may soon hear I am safe.

AIAS *exits by the side.* TEKMESSA *and*
EURYSAKES *reenter* AIAS' *tent.*

CHORUS   *second stasimon*

Desire thrills in me, joy gives me wings!   *strophe*   770
   Io Io Pan! Pan!
   Sail from the snow-whipped
   crags of Kyllene,
O dance-maker of the gods!
   Join us, launch me
   in the impulsive
dance, the ecstatic Knosian,
the Mysian step—now, now I want dancing!
   Come, Lord Apollo,
   from Delos, cross over   780
   the Icarian sea
in splendor, your favor stay with us now!

Rage has lifted its darkening terror.   *antistrophe*
   Io Io Zeus! Now
   white day dawns
   on our sea-sped ships!
For Aias has put pain away
   and gone in good mind
   to fulfill the saving
sacrifice to the gods.   790
Time truly is great, it quenches all things,
   nothing's too strange
   if Aias can turn
   his heart from hatred
and the huge struggle against the Atreidai.

MESSENGER *enters.*

MESSENGER Friends, I have messages. First,
Teukros just came back
from the mountains of Mysia, but he ran
into trouble by the generals' tent.
When the Greeks saw he was here,   800
they closed in, circling around him,
beating him down with insults—
no one stayed out of it—calling him
half-brother of a madman
and traitor to the army, threatening
to stone him to a bloody death.
There were swords drawn. It would have gone badly
if the elders had not spoken up
and stopped it.
                    But where is Aias?
I must make my report to him.   810
Your commander should know what's happened.

CHORUS He has just now gone, a new man
yoked to a new purpose.

MESSENGER Then I'm afraid I was sent too late
or took too long in coming.

CHORUS What do you mean? Why too late?

MESSENGER He was not to leave the tent.
He was to stay in and wait for Teukros.

CHORUS But he left in good mind, resolved
to end his anger at last   820
and make peace with the gods.

MESSENGER You're talking nonsense, if Kalchas
has any skill as a prophet.

CHORUS What do you know about it?

MESSENGER What I heard with my own ears. Kalchas
stepped out of the circle of leaders
alone, apart from the Atreidai.
He went over to Teukros, gave him
his right hand in friendship, and enjoined him
to keep Aias inside by all means,   830
absolutely forbid him to go out
for as long as this day's light lasts,
if he hoped to see him survive it.
The anger of the goddess Athene
will drive him for this day only.
So Kalchas declared. He said
the gods strike down unwieldy
and outsized bodies, men grown
from the human branch who let
their minds go beyond the human.   840
The man's father warned him against
such recklessness when he saw him
rushing headlong to war
with these noble words: "My son,
may your spear prevail over all,
but always with a god's protection."
But Aias answered with a high
and thoughtless boast: "My father,
any nobody can win victories
with the help of a god. I trust   850
I can draw enough glory to me
without them." That was the size of it.
Then a second time, when Athene
was urging him on in his deadly
work against the Trojans,
he turned to her and uttered
unspeakable words: "Go, mistress,
and stand by the rest of the Greeks.
The line won't break where I hold it."
What he gained with such crude talk   860
no man wants: the goddess's anger.
But if he outlives this day,
with the god's help we may save him.
      That is what Kalchas said.
I was sent at once to bring you
orders from Teukros and see them

carried out. If we're too late,
if what Kalchas said is true,
Aias is no more.

CHORUS   Tekmessa, born for all suffering,   870
come and hear this man's story!
It shaves too painfully close.

TEKMESSA and the boy enter from AIAS' *tent.*

TEKMESSA   Am I not wretched enough?
Must you call me out here again
when my troubles have just relented?

CHORUS   It was my own pain that called you.
Hear what he says about Aias.

TEKMESSA   What is it, man? Are we ruined?

MESSENGER   You may or may not be. My fear
is for Aias, if he has gone out.   880

TEKMESSA   He has gone out. Why do you frighten me?

MESSENGER   Teukros sent orders to keep him
under cover of his tent and not let him
go out alone.

TEKMESSA   Where is Teukros?
Why did he say these things?

MESSENGER   He has just returned. He thinks
that Aias may meet destruction
if he goes out there.

He points toward the fateful exit.

TEKMESSA   Ah, no!
What man told him that?

MESSENGER   The prophet
Kalchas. He says this day   890
means death or life for Aias.

TEKMESSA Ai! Help me, friends, protect me
against inescapable chance!
You, go and meet Teukros. Hurry!
The rest of you divide up and search
both the dawn and sunset arms
of the harbor. Find out where his dark will
has led him. He has deceived me,
I see it now, he has torn
all care for me from his heart.   900
Child, what shall I do? I can't
sit waiting, I must go with them
as far as my strength will let me.
Come all, let's be quick. The man
is in a hurry to die.

CHORUS No more words. We're ready.
Let the speed of our feet speak for us.

> The CHORUS *splits into two groups and exits by both sides.*
> ATTENDANTS *lead* EURYSAKES *back inside, as* TEKMESSA
> *hurries after one part of the* CHORUS.

> *The stage is emptied.*

> *The scene changes to a deserted part of the coast.*
> *The tent now represents a grove near the sea,*
> *the gates a small clearing out of which* AIAS *now*
> *appears on the wheeled platform. He stands over*
> *his sword which is buried point up in the ground.*

AIAS The killer, the sacrificial knife
is set now to be most cutting,
if there were time for such thoughts.   910
Hektor gave it to me, of all guest-friends
the man I most hated the sight of;
it stands in enemy earth,
Trojan earth, the edge newly ground
on the iron-eating stone,
planted firmly for one clean
and kindly stroke.
                     All is in order.
Zeus I call first, as is right,

not asking for some great prize,
but that you send the hard word   920
of this death to Teukros. Let him
be the first to find me and lift me
off of the streaming sword,
before my enemies come
and order my body cast out
to the dogs and crows. That is all
I ask of you, Zeus. And I call
on Hermes, guide of the underworld,
to take me down without struggle—
a quick leap, the sword's point breaking   930
up through my ribs.
                              And I call
on the everlasting virgins, the avengers
who see all mortal sufferings,
the dread, long-striding Furies,
to look at the wretched end
the Atreidai have brought me to.
Vile men! Come and take them!
And as you see me self-slaughtered,
so make them die vile deaths,
cut down by the hands of their dearest   940
offspring. Feed on them, you swift
and punishing Furies, feed
on the whole body of the army!
Spare none of them!
                              And you, Helios,
driving across the steep sky,
when you come to my homeland pull back
on the gold-flashed reins and report
this ruin and doom to my father
and the unhappy woman who nursed me.
When she hears it, her weeping will sound   950
through the whole city. But why
think of weeping—I must act quickly.
        O death, come, death, attend me
or I will come to you there.
O Helios, bright light of day,
I greet you one last time
and never again, O radiance!
O holy ground of Salamis,

hearth of my fathers, famous
Athens, and our one people,   9●
springs, rivers, and the wide plain
of Troy—you have all sustained me.
Farewell! Aias calls out
his last word to you. The rest
I will speak to the dead in Hades.

*The platform is wheeled back, disappearing into the
grove as* AIAS *speaks his last words. There is a pause.*

The two parts of the CHORUS
rush on stage from both sides.

CHORUS A   Pain brings pain more pain.
                     I've searched, searched
                 everywhere and everywhere the place
                        has kept its secret.
                 Listen! A noise! Who is there?   970

CHORUS B Your shipmates.

CHORUS A   What news?

CHORUS B   We searched
                 the whole west side of the harbor.

CHORUS A And found?

CHORUS B   Much work, nothing more.

CHORUS A Nor has he come to light
                 anywhere on the eastern side.

    CHORUS   *strophe*
                 If only some labor-loving
                 son of the sea at his sleepless
                     hunt, some nymph
                        of the hills or the quick-
                 flowing Bosphorus who can see   980
                 where the raw-hearted man

57

          is wandering now
          would call out and tell us! For me
          this toiling aimlessness
          is a hard thing, with no wind-
          blown speed, no sight of fleeting Aias.

TEKMESSA   Io moi moi!

CHORUS Who cried out by that grove?

TEKMESSA   No, no, no!

         The gates open and the elevated platform is wheeled out
           with TEKMESSA *kneeling over, and partially blocking,*
                AIAS' *body from view.*

CHORUS I see her, Tekmessa, the captive,   990
          the young wife, stricken with grief.

TEKMESSA All is ended, all destroyed for me, friends!

CHORUS   What is it?

TEKMESSA Aias is here, newly killed—
         his body draped over his sword.

CHORUS   Omoi, no homecoming!
         Oh, I am cut down, too,
         lord, your luckless shipmate!
          Such suffering, woman!

TEKMESSA He's dead! Weep for him! Ah, Aias!   1000

CHORUS But how, who, whose hand did it?

TEKMESSA His own. The sword he fell on,
         stuck here in the ground, convicts him.

CHORUS   Oh, my blindness! Alone, your life bleeding
         away, no friend there
         to prevent you! And I, dull-witted, all
         unheeding, to fail so!

Where is he, where is intractable
Aias, named to no good end?

TEKMESSA He must not be seen! I will cover
his body, I will wrap him completely
in my mantle. No one who loved him
could bear to see the dark blood
pouring from his nostrils and the raw
wound his own hand made.

TEKMESSA *enshrouds the body of* AIAS.

Oh, what must I do now?
Which friend should lift you up?
Where is Teukros? If only he'd come
in time at least to help me
prepare his brother for burial!   1020
Ah, to lie fallen here was no fate
for a man like you, Aias!
Even your enemies would weep to see it.

CHORUS   *antistrophe*
It had to have happened in time,
stiff heart, you had to have brought
    your boundless agony
    to this fulfillment.
I see it now. Night long and day long
your mind raged, your bright hatred cried out
    against the Atreidai.   1030
How else could such deadly passion
have ended? Time, since the best men
contended for the arms of Achilles,
has been a potent begetter of sorrows

TEKMESSA   Io moi moi!

CHORUS True grief goes to the heart.

TEKMESSA   Io moi moi!

CHORUS I don't wonder that you cry out twice
in pain for so dear a loss.

TEKMESSA You see how it seems, but I know it.   1040

CHORUS   You are right.

TEKMESSA Oh, child, what a yoke of slavery
         we're bound for, what cold-eyed masters!

CHORUS   No! What you say
         is unthinkable, that the ruthless
         Atreidai would add still more to your grief!
         May god prevent it!

TEKMESSA Is this not the gods' work?

CHORUS   Yes,
         they've laid an unbearable weight on you.

TEKMESSA It's the sort of bane the dreaded   1050
         daughter of Zeus will breed
         for the sake of her dear Odysseus.

CHORUS   What outrage that much-enduring
                   man commits
         in his black heart! He laughs a great laugh
                   at these frenzied calamities,
         and the double-ruling Atreidai
         listen and laugh with him!

TEKMESSA Let them laugh, then, let them rejoice
         at his destruction! They had   1060
         no use for him alive, but now
         in the press of battle they may well
         lament his death. Evil-minded
         men never see what good
         they have till they've thrown it away.
                   His death is more bitter for me
         than sweet for them, but for him
         it is joy. The end he so passionately
         yearned for, he brought about
         by himself. What can they laugh at?   1070
         He died by the gods, not by them. No!
                   Let Odysseus hurl his useless

60

insults, Aias won't hear them.
He is as far from their laughter
as he is now from my grief.

TEUKROS   Io moi moi!

CHORUS Listen! I think that was Teukros.
The tune of his cry goes straight
to the mark of this ruin.

                    TEUKROS *and* ATTENDANTS *enter in haste.*

TEUKROS   Aias!
Dear brother, bright eye of my blood!   1080
Have you done as rumor says?

CHORUS The man is dead, Teukros.

TEUKROS   Ai!
A heavy fate bears down on me!

CHORUS So it is.

TEUKROS   Ah, woe for me!

CHORUS You're right to lament.

TEUKROS   It breaks over me!

CHORUS Yes, it is terrible, and sudden.

TEUKROS The boy, his son, where is he
in all this Trojan country?

CHORUS Alone by the tents.

TEUKROS   Find him, then,
and bring him here, or some enemy   1090
may snatch him up like a lion cub
strayed from its mother. Go,
go quickly, help him! Believe me,

men love to mock the dead
when they have them at their feet.

                                        TEKMESSA *exits.*

CHORUS   That is well done, Teukros. His final
         order was for you to take care
         of the boy, as you're doing now.

TEUKROS Oh, of all my eyes have seen
         this is the most painful sight.   1100
         No other road I've walked
         has torn my guts the way this road
         did, oh, Aias, when I learned
         it was your death I was tracking.
              Word of it cut through the Greeks
         with godly suddenness. Hearing it
         before I could reach you, I groaned.
         But now I see, and the sight
         destroys me! Ai! Uncover him,
         let me look at the whole evil.   1110

         AIAS *is revealed, impaled face up on his sword.*

              Oh, bitter sight, that hard face,
         that grim self-command! What griefs
         you've sown for me with your death!
         Where can I go, among what men,
         when I was no help to you
         in your struggle? Oh, yes, Telamon,
         your father and mine, will meet me
         with pleasant smiles when I come home
         without you. Of course! The man
         never smiled at the best of luck.   1120
         What will he hold back, what vile names
         will he not turn against me—bastard
         gotten by a hostile spear, coward,
         weakling who let you die
         out of fear—oh, Aias, my brother!
         Or he'll say I betrayed you to get
         your place and power on Salamis.
         Ill-tempered, quarrelsome, overbearing

old man! I'll be banished, driven out
with his word—*slave*—on my head.
That waits for me at home, while here
at Troy I have enemies everywhere
and little help. So much
for the good your death has done me!
    What now? How can I drag you
from that bright, biting sword-point,
the slayer that took your last breath?
Did you see that Hektor would finally
destroy you, even though he was dead?
    By the gods, look at the fates   1140
of these two men! With the wide belt
that Aias gave him, Hektor
was lashed to the chariot and dragged,
mangled, till the spirit left him.
Aias took this sword in gift
from Hektor and died falling on it.
Was it the Furies who forged this sword?
Did that savage workman Hades
fashion the belt? Not just these things,
I say, but all fates always   1150
are worked against men by the gods.
Whoever has no stomach
for my words can look for comfort
in his own thoughts. Those are mine.

CHORUS Don't stretch this talk any further.
You had better think how to get him
buried, and what you will say next.
I see someone coming, an enemy,
no straight-hearted man, I'm afraid,
who may mean to laugh at our suffering.   1160

TEUKROS Which one of the army is it?

CHORUS Menelaos, whom we sailed here to help.

TEUKROS I see him now. From this distance
it is not hard to tell who he is.

MENELAOS *enters with* ARMED ATTENDANTS.

MENELAOS You, keep your hands off that corpse,
          I order you! Do not try to lift it.

TEUKROS Those are big words—what stands behind them?

MENELAOS My judgment, and the chief commander's.

TEUKROS On what grounds, may I ask?

MENELAOS We brought him here thinking he was   1170
          a friend and ally. We've learned
          that he was a more dangerous enemy
          than any Trojan, a traitor
          who plotted to murder our army
          and came in the night against us
          to cut us down. One of the gods
          blocked his attack, otherwise
          the disgrace of this death, which is his lot,
          would have fallen to us, and he
          would be alive now. As it happened,   1180
          the god turned his outrage on shepherds
          and sheep.
                        I say throw him out!
          No man, not one of you here,
          has the power to put him in a grave.
          Let him lie on the yellow sand
          somewhere and feed sea birds. And you,
          don't work yourself up against us.
          I grant you, we failed to control him
          when he was alive, but he's dead now,
          and like it or not we will have   1190
          our way with him. At no time, so long
          as the breath was in him, would he ever
          obey me.
                        Indeed, it's a mark
          of baseness in a man from the ranks
          to deny the need for obedience.
          Can laws keep the city on a prosperous
          course if no one fears them?
          In the same way, an army cannot
          be governed wisely without
          a strong bulwark of fear and respect.   1200

For however large a man grows,
he must bear in mind that one small
defect can bring him down.
Where fear and shame come together
in a man, they act to preserve him.
But where there is wantonness
and license, the city, though she
be speeding before a fair wind,
will plunge to destruction. Fear
is the cornerstone of all order,   1110
I say. We should not take pleasure
and deny pain equal measure.
One comes on the other's heels.
Not long ago this man blazed
with insolence. Now it is I
who have big ideas, so I warn you:
if you dig a grave for him,
you yourselves may fall into it.

CHORUS Menelaos, you have spoken wisely
of restraint. Do not outrage the dead.   1220

TEUKROS Why should it surprise me, friends,
when a man of no birth does wrong,
if one presumed to be noble
can speak such twisted words?
        Let me hear it again. You say
you brought him here, you yourself,
as an ally of the Greeks? He came
under his own sails, you know that!
What right could you have to command him
or the men he led from home?   1230
Your power extends to the Spartans,
not to us. Nothing ever gave you
any claim to rule him, or him you.
In fact, you came here under orders,
not as general of us all.
You command Aias? Rule the men
you're entitled to rule, punish them
with your pompous talk. Your mouth
does not frighten me. Forbid it,
get the other general to forbid it—   1240

I will bury Aias
as justice demands. He did not join
this expedition for the sake
of your wife, like the drudges you brought here,
but because of oaths he had sworn.
And not because of you. He never
honored nonentities.
                                        Go on, then,
bring more heralds, bring the commander
himself. All your noise will not sway me
as long as you are what you are.   1250

CHORUS We have trouble enough without
these sharp words. Even if they're true,
they cut too deep.

MENELAOS   The archer
has a high opinion of himself.

TEUKROS I am not ashamed of my skill.

MENELAOS He'd boast more if he carried a shield.

TEUKROS I'll match all your bronze barehanded.

MENELAOS Can your heart be as fierce as your tongue?

TEUKROS As proud as my cause is just.

MENELAOS It is just to defend a killer?   1260

TEUKROS How strange, to be killed and yet living!

MENELAOS A god saved me, but in his mind
I was dead.

TEUKROS   So the gods saved you
and now you dishonor the gods?

MENELAOS What divine laws have I broken?

TEUKROS You hinder the burial of the dead.

MENELAOS I am right in that. We were enemies.

TEUKROS When did Aias oppose you in battle?

MENELAOS You know we hated each other.

TEUKROS He had good reason to hate you.   1270
He knew you fixed the vote.

MENELAOS It fell as the judges decided.

TEUKROS You could put a good face on your cheating.

MENELAOS Those words may cause someone pain.

TEUKROS No worse for me than for you.

MENELAOS I tell you Aias will not
be buried!

TEUKROS   I tell you he will!

MENELAOS I saw a man once whose bold talk
had pressed a ship's crew to set sail
in winter. A storm broke, the waves   1280
piled higher and higher, and he
grew quieter and quieter, huddled
in the stern under his cloak. The sailors
stepped on him in the confusion
and he said nothing at all.
So, if a great storm blows up
from a small cloud, it may silence
your big voice in the same way.

TEUKROS I, too, saw a man once, full
of his own stupidity, who insulted   1290
his neighbors in their grief.
Someone who looked like me,
and was like me in temper, warned him:
"Man, do not outrage the dead.
If you do, it will be your own ruin."
So the fool was told to his face.

I can still see him now: I think
he's none other than you, Menelaos!
Am I talking in riddles?

MENELAOS   Enough!
It's shameful for me to trade insults   1300
with you when I can use force.

MENELAOS and ATTENDANTS *exit.*

TEUKROS   Creep away! It's shameful for me
to waste time on your empty words!

CHORUS   A struggle is coming, a great strife.
Hurry, Teukros, find some hollow
trench to serve as his dank tomb—
rotting earth to receive his body,
his memorial among men everlasting.

TEKMESSA and EURYSAKES *enter and
approach* AIAS' *body.*

TEUKROS   See, now, his near ones are coming,
his son and wife, when we   1310
most need them to perform the rites
for these poor remains.

Mother and son strike a pose of formal supplication.

                          Come, child,
kneel here and touch the body
of the father who gave you life.
Come, hold on to him. Keep
a lock of my hair in your hand,
a lock of your mother's hair,
and a third lock of your own.
This is a suppliant's treasure.
And if anyone comes from the army   1320
to drag you away from this corpse,
may the wretch be cast out, unburied,
cut off with the whole of his race,
as I cut off this lock of hair!
Hold on to him, child. Guard him.

Let no one move you. And you,
remember you're men, not serving girls!
Defend him until I come back.
I'll go and prepare a grave for him
whether they permit it or not.   1330

                                    TEUKROS *exits.*

                  TEKMESSA *and* EURYSAKES *remain as suppliants*
                                       beside the body of AIAS.

CHORUS   *third stasimon*
            What year? I wish I knew   *strophe*
what year will be the last of my wandering
years and waves of spear-driven, ruinous
            toil coming against me
            over the plains of Troy,
bringing bitter disgrace to the Greeks.

            The man who invented war,   *antistrophe*
if only he had vanished in the steep sky or sunk
to the common darkness of Hades before
            he taught men to use the tools   1340
            of hateful, heedless Ares —
oh, pain breeding pain — for the slaughter of men.

            He has robbed me of garlands   *strophe*
            and deep wine bowls,
kept me far from the joy of friendship, the sweet
            clamor of flutes,
            he has cut me off
                from the night-
                long joys
            of sleep and love and lovemaking,   1350
            Ai, I'm abandoned out here
            with thick dew soaking my hair,
            a constant, cold reminder
                of alien Troy.

            Once my great wall   *antistrophe*
            against weapons and terrors
under the pall of night was relentless Aias.
            He lies here now

offered up to the baleful
    force of his fate.   1360
    What joy
have I left? Oh, I wish I were sailing
past the wooded rampart of Sounion
where the rock juts into the sea,
and shouting out my praises
    to holy Athens.

                      TEUKROS *enters in haste.*

TEUKROS Look there, it's Agamemnon!
    I turned back when I saw him coming.
    He'll let his crude tongue loose now!

        AGAMEMNON *enters with great pomp, accompanied*
                by MENELAOS *and* ARMED ATTENDANTS.

AGAMEMNON Teukros! I've heard some amazing   1370
    reports about you. Do you think
    you can talk so boldly against us
    and go unpunished? A slave's son?
    No doubt if your mother was noble
    you'd boast even higher, prancing
    around on the tips of your toes!
    What does all this defiance amount to?
    A nobody defending nothing!
    So you claim that we're not generals,
    not captains of ships for the Greeks,   1380
    not for you? And that Aias sailed here
    under his own command?
    Is it not monstrous to hear
    such things from a slave?

                    Who is
    this man you're bellowing about?
    Where has he stood in battle
    that I was not standing with him?
    Are there no other men in the army?
    Oh, it was a bad day for us,
    the day we declared the contest   1390
    for Achilles' armor. Now Teukros
    denounces us everywhere,
    unable to yield to what

the majority of judges decided
and accept defeat. You were beaten,
and now, like others of your kind,
you turn to insults and treachery.
No laws can stand firm if we drive out
the rightful victors and bring
men up from behind to replace them.   1400
    Such tendencies must be checked!
It's a wise mind, not a broad back,
that prevails. An ox, for all
its great girth, is driven down the road
with a little whip. You may feel
the sting of that treatment yourself
if you cannot listen to reason.
Behind all this outrage and loud talk
what is there? A man who's no more
than a shadow!
                    Know your place, Teukros.   1410
And since you lack the qualities
of a free man, bring someone else
to plead your case for you.
I can learn nothing from your way
of talking. Such barbarous speech
is foreign to my ears.

CHORUS You both should listen to reason,
        that is the best I can say.

TEUKROS Hah! a man dies, and how quickly
         all gratitude fades and is lost   1420
         in betrayal! Oh, Aias, you count
         for nothing in this man's memory,
         though you laid your life out so often
         toiling with your spear for him.
         It's all gone, all thrown away now.
             You who just spoke so many
         and such thoughtless words, can it be
         you've forgotten the time you were driven
         behind your own walls in a rout
         of spears? Your war was lost,   1430
         but he came alone and saved you.
         And when fire was already licking

at the stern rails of our ships,
and Hektor leaped over the trenches
among the black hulls, who stopped him?
Was it not this man? Were you
standing with him, as you say?
He did what was right. And again,
he met Hektor in single combat—
not on your orders. They drew lots.   1440
Did Aias put in a wet lump
of earth that would sink to the bottom?
No, he put in the lightest
bit of clay, and when the plumed helmet
was shaken, it leaped to the top.
That's the sort of man he was.
And I was beside him, the slave,
the barbarian woman's son.

    Wretched man, where are you looking
when you taunt me with that? Wasn't Pelops,   1450
you father's father, a barbarian
Phrygian? And what about Atreus,
who sowed your seed? What unholy
meal did he serve his brother?
The man's own children! Your mother
was a Cretan woman, who was caught
by her father making love
with a stranger and sent to her death
among speechless fish. And you
insult me? I am Telamon's son.   1460
His consort, my mother, was royal—
Laomedon's daughter. He received her
as the highest prize for valor
from Alkmene's son, Herakles.
Having sprung from two such noble
parents, how could I bring
dishonor on a man of my blood
who has fallen, whose corpse you shamelessly
order to be left unburied!

    I warn you, if you cast him out,   1470
you must cast out the bodies of us three
as well. It would be much nobler
for me to die here in the light
for his sake, than to die for that woman

72

of yours, or I should say your brother's.
Look to your own affairs
and leave mine to me. If you cross me,
you'll find it would have been better
to be a coward than to act so boldly.

ODYSSEUS *enters.*

CHORUS Lord Odysseus, you have come at need,   1480
if you mean to loosen this struggle
and not to bind it tighter.

ODYSSEUS Men, what is happening here?
From far off I heard the Atreidai
shouting over this brave corpse.

AGAMEMNON And we, Lord Odysseus, have just heard
outrageous talk from this man.

ODYSSEUS How, outrageous? I understand
a man who meets insults with anger.

AGAMEMNON Yes, he has listened to insults,   1490
because he has acted against me

ODYSSEUS Indeed? What harm has he done you?

AGAMEMNON He says he will not leave this corpse
without its portion of earth.
He will bury him, in defiance of me!

ODYSSEUS Can a friend speak the truth and still
pull his oar beside you?

AGAMEMNON   Speak
I would be foolish not to listen
to my chief friend of all the Greek host.

ODYSSEUS Hear me then. Before the gods,   1500
do not dare to cast this man out
unburied, so callously! Never
let violence drive you so far

73

in your hate that you tread on justice.
I, too, found him hateful once,
more than any other man,
after I won the armor of Achilles.
But though he held to his enmity,
I would not repay him now
with dishonor, or deny that in my eyes   1510
he was the greatest of all
who came to Troy, second only
to Achilles. If you dishonor him,
there can be no justice in it.
You will not harm him, you will harm
the laws of the gods. To strike
at a brave man when he is dead
can never be just, no matter
how much you hate him.

AGAMEMNON   Odysseus,
                 you are fighting for him against me!   1520

ODYSSEUS Yes, though when honor demanded,
         I hated him.

AGAMEMNON   Does honor not tell you
               to trample him now that he's dead?

ODYSSEUS Do not glory, son of Atreus,
         in such an ill-gotten advantage.

AGAMEMNON A ruler does not always find it
          easy to be pious.

ODYSSEUS   But it's not hard
             to honor a friend's good advice.

AGAMEMNON A good man should yield to authority.

ODYSSEUS Enough of that! You can prevail   1530
             by giving way to your friends.

AGAMEMNON Remember who you are asking
          this favor for!

ODYSSEUS   My enemy,
it's true, yet once he was noble.

AGAMEMNON And you mean to show such respect
to an enemy's corpse?

ODYSSEUS   Yes.
I am moved more by his greatness
than by my enmity.

AGAMEMNON I distrust such unstable natures.

ODYSSEUS I assure you, most men are that way,   1540
now friendly, now hostile.

AGAMEMNON   And are these
the sort of friends you would praise?

ODYSSEUS I would not praise an obstinate mind!

AGAMEMNON You will make us look like cowards.

ODYSSEUS Not cowards but men of justice —
so all the Greeks will call you.

AGAMEMNON I must let them bury the body,
is that what you say?

ODYSSEUS   It is.
I will face the same need some day.

AGAMEMNON It's all one, then, and each man works   1550
for himself.

ODYSSEUS   There is reason in that.
Who else should I work for?

AGAMEMNON   Well, then,
let it be your decision, not mine.

ODYSSEUS Either way you will do what is right.

75

AGAMEMNON If you asked for a much greater favor,
               I would grant it, be sure of that.
               As for him, he is hateful to me
               whether he lies on the earth or under it.
               Do what's necessary with the body.

AGAMEMNON, MENELAOS, *and* ARMED ATTENDANTS *exit.*

CHORUS There is wisdom in you, Odysseus.   1560
           Whoever denies it is a fool.

ODYSSEUS Now let me say to Teukros
           that as much as I was his enemy
           before, I will be his friend
           from this day on. If he will,
           I would like to share with you
           in the work and the rites of burial,
           leaving out nothing that a mortal
           can do for the best of men.

TEUKROS You're a noble man, Odysseus.   1570
           I praise you for all that you've said.
           How greatly I misjudged you!
           The man he most hated was the one man
           of all the Greeks who stood by him,
           and would not endure while he lived
           to see outrage done to the dead—
           to leave him unburied, defiled,
           as those two, the thundering general
           and his blood brother wanted. For that
           may the father who rules Olympos,   1580
           the remembering Furies, and all-
           fulfilling Justice bring them
           to as vile an end as they wished
           for him!
                   But, son of Laertes,
           I cannot let you touch his body,
           for fear of offending the dead.
           You may take part in the rest.
           If you bring others from the army
           to honor him, that will be well.

I must work now. What you have done   1590
is noble. We will not forget it.

ODYSSEUS I wished to help, but with all
respect for your thoughts, I will leave.

Exit ODYSSEUS.

TEUKROS   exodos
Come, too much time has passed already.
We must dig the grave, set the tall tripod
up and the caldron ringed with fire
for the sacred bath. Bring his arms from the tent
in trophy, covered by the great shield.
I need your love and your small strength, child
Help me to lift your father gently,   1600
the black life force is still flowing out
of his warm veins. Come, you who called him friend,
and work for this man's sake, who was noble
in all that he did. For while Aias lived,
I say there was no better man in the world.

TEUKROS, EURYSAKES *and the* CHORUS, *who now*
approach the elevated platform, lift the body of
AIAS *off the sword.*

CHORUS Mortals know what their eyes can see,
but of what will come out of time there is
no seeing, no knowing what the end will be.

All exit in procession bearing the body of AIAS.

NOTES ON THE TEXT
GLOSSARY

NOTES ON THE TEXT

TIME AND PLACE

The wooden stage building (*skene*) represents Aias' camp; the central, double doors, or gates, lead to his quarters. Two side entrances, one of which was probably used to represent the "Greek" side, that is, the side leading to and from the Greek camp, and the other the side by which Aias and those close to him come and go, visually reenforce the play's thematic polarities. As the tracking scene suggests, the time is very likely dawn, the traditional starting time of the day's first play. Since the Theater of Dionysos was open, the dramatist made "the world" his stage. The reader should try to visualize the effect: day dawns as the strange tracks leading to Aias become clear. By involving the natural world in his drama, Sophocles creates an immediate sense of the cosmic scope of Aias' tragedy. (Compare Aeschylus' use of dawning light to dramatize the world-dimension of his *Agamemnon*.)

STRUCTURE OF THE PLAY

The play is, like all Greek plays, made up of spoken dialogue, mono logues, choral lyrics, and lyric exchanges. "Acts," encounters, and speeches involving the principal characters are divided by lyrical interludes sung and danced by the chorus. Scholars regularly refer to the speeches and/or dialogue preceding the entrance of the chorus as the "prologue," the choral entrance song as the "*parodos*" (162 ff.), the exchanges between the principals as "episodes," and the choral songs as "*stasima*" (stasimon in the singular). The lyric parts of the play are evenly distributed between choral song, of which there are four, and lyric dialogues, of which there are three. We should note several things about the structure of this play. First, all but one of the choral *stasima* occur in the first half of the play (the significance of which is discussed in the Introduction). Second, there is also a relatively high concentration of (dramatically heightening) lyric dialogue in the first half of the play, that is, sung exchanges (in lyric meter) between a principal character, such as Tekmessa or Aias, and the chorus, who become a virtual second actor in the first part of the drama. In other words, the lyric structure of this play is quite intricate, and so the balance of spoken and sung parts should be taken into consideration when thinking about the dramatic effects, mood, tone, and feeling of the play.

1–161 *prologue*

1–16 *I always see . . . what I know.* Is Athene actually visible? Odysseus states that he can hear but not see her. If the goddess is present (presumably, she would appear above on the *theologeion*, literally the place for "god-speech," on the roof of the *skene*), Sophocles visually confronts his audience with a contrast between Aias' and Odysseus' perspectives. Aias, blinded by Athene, nonetheless sees her. Odysseus, her favorite and the character in Homer who most often sees Athene when others do not, here cannot see her. Physically and metaphysically, Sophocles suggests the two men are very different. Like so much else in this play, the scene is unparalleled. The scene perhaps glances at *Iliad* 1.194 ff., where Athene appears to Achilles to stay him from shedding Greek blood. But Athene's intervention there produces honor, not humiliation. This daimonic Athene is finally unlike anything in Sophocles, closer in fact to a Euripidean goddess, a divine *alastōr*, like Aphrodite in the *Hippolytos*.

1 *I always* Always (*aei*) is the first word of the play, and the first of many temporal expressions. Always (sometimes rendered forever in our text) is Aias' word, the voice of his *daimon* (e.g., 141, 373, 641). The play is concerned with "time," divine permanence vs. human transience, even in the subtlest details of its language.

4 *around where Aias* Aias is his Greek name. Despite the familiar Latinized form, Ajax, we have used the Greek form throughout. Chiefly for reasons of sound. The Greek name suggests a cry of pain, which is dramatically exploited by Sophocles (see 468).

10 *sharp-nosed Spartan bitch* The keenness of Spartan hounds was proverbial.

19–20 *your words ring like a bronze-mouthed / trumpet* Athene was said to have invented the first trumpet; the instrument was also blown in the Theater of Dionysos at the beginning of a play. Perhaps these words confirm that the trumpet blows as Athene begins speaking her prologue.

22 *the great shield.* A warrior's arms were an intrinsic part of his identity. Hektor had his helmet, with its "frightfully nodding horse-hair crest"; Achilles, his "divine" armor and the Pelian ash spear that only he could lift. Aias was famous for his huge, seven-layered, ox-hide shield. His colossal size together with his shield made him Homer's "bulwark of the Greeks."

48–49 *Rage / over the award of Achilles' armor.* Achilles' armor, described in Book 18 *of the Iliad*, was made for him by the god Hephaistos. "Immortal": the armor shone so brilliantly that Achilles' enemies were nearly blinded by it. It was in this armor that Achilles avenged the death of Patroklos and won his *aristeia* (heroic glory).

56 *He came stalking you in the darkness.* Crafty Odysseus is the hero chosen by the Greeks for "night-raiding." In *Iliad* 10, he and Diomedes kill many sleeping Phrygians. But such an act is totally out of character for Aias, whose single combat with Hektor stops promptly at nightfall (*Iliad* 7.282 ff.).

93 *And is any laughter sweeter* To laugh at your enemy's misfortune is part of ancient Greek morality: love your friends and hate your enemies. The precept was still acceptable in Sophoclean Athens; not seriously challenged before Plato, it might be argued that Odysseus here anticipates Plato's challenge to it. Derisive laughter or fear of laughter haunt the play. Aias, Tekmessa, the chorus, all fear that Aias has become a laughing-stock.

145–46 *greater foresight . . . shifts of action?* This is unexpected. Aias, the "great bulwark of the Achaians," is known for relentlessness in battle, not especially for his "foresight" or "timeliness in action" (literally what the Greek says). He is once called "wise" by Hektor (*Iliad* 7.288 f.), but this is at an unusually gracious moment. This is perhaps the first hint, along with the allusions to the brightness of Aias' eyes (84; 101), that Sophocles' Aias is not the merely lumbering hulk of tradition.

158–59 *One day can . . . all human things.* Another image of man's ephemerality. The metaphor in Greek is one of balance scales and comes from Homer's image of Zeus weighing men's fates. The novelty here is that the "day" metaphorically becomes the scale (compare Aias' description of time as a succession of days moving back and forth, 523 ff.). Using the same metaphor, Athene identifies divine pleasure and displeasure with the vagaries of Time (also compare lines 834 f.).

162–220 *parodos* (choral entrance song) The choral range of expression runs from spoken dialogue to chant to full song. Distinctions between song and chant should be obvious from shifts in tone, and are noted in stage directions, when, as in this *parodos*, the difference between them seems an important part of Sophocles' dramatic texture. Note, for example, the shifts in emotional level as the chorus enter in a discursive mode, chanting 162–91; then invoke the gods and Aias in lyric 192–220; then address Tekmessa, whom they first question in chant 228–32, and then afterwards in song, when she has told them about Aias, 240–50, 263–73; finally, also note the chorus's first "spoken" words after the lyric intensity has abated: "But fortunately it is over" (280), referring to the assault of Aias' madness, with which their lyric excitement has kept pace. The choral leader "spoke" for the chorus in ancient practice.

189 *let a great eagle* Aias, according to Pindar (*Isthmian* 6.63 ff.), was named after the eagle—*Aias* from *aietos*. Sophocles conjures up the eagle glare but carefully avoids using Pindar's etymology. Instead, he uses the more unusual *aigupion* (normally meaning "vulture") for "eagle," which sounds nothing like *Aias*.

209 *race of Sisyphos* An alternative (and pejorative) genealogy of Odysseus, normally son of Laertes (as in the *Odyssey* and in *Aias* 120). Sisyphos was king of Corinth and infamous for cunning and deceit.

221–673 first *episode*

222 *earth-born race of Erechtheus* Allusion to the autochthony of the Athenians, who regarded themselves descendants of "earth-born" Erechtheus. Sophocles is here assuming the identity of the Salaminian sailors as Athenians, which Aias (958 f.) and the chorus (1362 ff.) will again reenforce.

227 *afflicted by a darkening storm.* Literally, turbid or "muddy" storm. Traditionally, the madness is described as an "insane flashing" (words of the physician and skilled diagnostician, Podaleirius, from the *Aithiopis*) in his eyes. Sophocles describes Aias' madness with images of darkness, his recovery with images of light.

261–62 *a daimon / must have spoken through him.* Though our word "demon" comes from *daimon*, the two are not to be confused. The Greek word can mean several things: a man's "destiny" (as in Latin, *genius*) or a "divine being" (the two are not always mutually exclusive in Greek experience). It is quite often used, as here, indefinitely—that is, when the speaker senses the presence of the divine but not of a particular divinity.

274 *The way flashing lightning* The Greek literally says, "as swift south wind having darted ceases *without flashing lightning.*" Numerous attempts have been made to explain this strange phrase.

320–22 *broke their necks . . . to the bone.* Almost unutterably alliterative and ono-matopoeic in Greek: *euchenidze . . . esphadze karrachidze.* All the rhetorical stops are pulled in these speeches relating an offstage horror. The effect is sensory preparation for the greater horror to come. In this case, the appearance of Aias sprawled in the carnage: the vision of an Homeric hero turned mad butcher.

360 *Friends may win their friends back.* The Homeric Aias also honored friendship. Compare *Iliad* 9.641–42 where it forms the basis of his appeal to Achilles.

362–64 *man's misfortunes . . . possession.* Literally, "possessed by Apollo." Aias is, in a sense, about to become Apollo's creature: insight and then revelation follow his madness. For the confluence of Apollo's visionary gifts and madness consider the case of Cassandra in Aeschylus' *Agamemnon.*

380–464 *kommos* (dirge)

380–464 *Io! / Shipmates, friends . . . in filth and dishonor!* In the usual *kommos* a principal character and the chorus engage in lyric dialogue; here only Aias sings in lyric meter, whereas the chorus and Tekmessa respond with spoken dialogue. Compare 240–79, a lyric exchange between Tekmessa and the chorus.

422 f. *O Zeus, father* Zeus was Aias' great-grandfather. The genealogy is: Zeus, Aiakos, Telamon, Aias.

441–42 *My honor is dead . . . as these creatures.* These lines are obscure in Greek. Aias seems to be referring to "something" that has perished, which is contrasted with his "present state." We prefer the reading in the manuscripts (now accepted by Lloyd-Jones and Wilson, the editors of the most recent OCT edition of the play [Oxford 1990]), which can mean "these creatures."

468 *Aiai! My name is a lament!* In Sophocles, name is sometimes destiny: Oedipus, "swollen-foot" and "knowing one"; Philoctetes, "possessor of friends." This "tragic" etymology is Sophocles' innovation.

473–76 *For I am a man . . . most beautiful spoils* Telamon stormed Troy with his friend Herakles after King Laomedon refused to reward them for rescuing his daughter, Hesione, from a sea serpent. Herakles gave Hesione, the highest prize of honor, to Telamon. She became the mother of Aias' half-brother Teukros. Before their expedition to Troy, according to some accounts, Heracles prayed that Telamon should have an invincible son. Zeus' eagle, for which Aias was named (see note at 189), appeared as an omen and Aias was born to Eriboia. Both the contrast with his father and the new etymology of his name remind the audience how far Aias has fallen. Aias actually speaks of the prize as most "beautiful," which is a fifth-century anachronism, where *kalos*, "beauty," connotes moral as well as physical sublimity. He uses a similar expression at lines 530–31 when he speaks of "Honor in life / or in death."

482 f. *if Achilles himself* After losing the armor that was stripped from Patroklos by the Trojans, Achilles says that he could wear no man's armor except Aias' (*Iliad* 18.192).

494 *grim-eyed gorgopis*, literally "Gorgon-eyed," a contemptuous substitute for Athene's regular epithet, *glaukopis*, "gray-eyed." Athene wore the Gorgon head in the center of her shield, which she doubtless carried with her in the prologue.

522 *not born gutless.* The word in Greek is *asplagchnos.* The *splangchnon*, "innards," was regarded as the seat of deep emotion and heroic spirit. When he learns of Aias' death, Teukros will use the same term (1102).

523–33 *To stretch your . . . all there is to say.* The lines are striking and contain an unusual image from a board game, that of pieces moved forward and backward.

530–32 *Honor in life . . . or the other.* The literal sense is "to live nobly (*kalos*), to die nobly is necessary for the well-born (*eugene*) man." *Kalos* and *eugenes* were the fifth-century moral equivalents of the Homeric *arista / aristos* (best).

538 ff. *there is no greater evil* In Sophocles, the hero's moderate-minded foil, the *sōphrōn*, always argues for accepting "inevitable chance," whatever form it may take. Jocasta (*Oedipus the King*) urges Oedipus to live "at random." Deianeira (*Women of Trachis*) argues that men must submit to the vagaries of ineluctable eros. This is tragic wisdom, the kind of "human thoughts" that the messenger says that Aias rejects (836 ff.). The hero is by nature a metaphysical malcontent who cannot, like other men, accept limits. Both hero and *sōphrōn* are essential to Sophocles' vision, and his drama draws much of its power from the tension between these two opposed—and yet interdependent—types.

540–86 *My father was . . . cannot be noble.* Tekmessa's speech closely resembles that of Andromache to Hektor at *Iliad* 6.406–39, the epic prototype of the departure scene here. As in Andromache's case ("Hektor . . . you are father to me . . . mother . . . brother, and husband") the appeal is particularly strong because of the totality of her dependence upon Aias—he is mother, father, wealth, and homeland. One interesting difference is Tekmessa's assertion that it will be to Aias' "shame" if he dies. Compare Tekmessa's words at 557–61 with the following words, not of Andromache but of *Hektor*: "This is the wife of Hektor, greatest warrior / of the horse-breaking men of Troy . . . so someone will say of you; and for you it will hurt again to be widowed of such a man . . ." (6.460–63) Aias' gruffness is markedly different from the tenderness of Hektor, whose words to Andromache are perhaps the gentlest in the *Iliad* (esp. 6.450–65).

575–76 *My homeland / vanished* No pre-Sophoclean version of Aias' destruction of Tekmessa's homeland, Phrygia, is known. Andromache (see note at 540–86) makes the same point to Hektor, but it was Achilles, not her husband, who destroyed her homeland. Although she evokes Aias' violent pillaging of her country, Tekmessa also implies, at the end of her speech, a real intimacy between her and Aias.

609 ff. *Lift him up to me.* Parallel to the Homeric scene of Hektor with his young son, Astyanax (6.466–81). The implicit contrast between Aias and Hektor is strong, for example, in their respective addresses to their sons. When Hektor raised his son in his arms, the boy cried out in terror at the sight of his father's famous bronze helmet with its dreadfully nodding crest. Laughing, Hektor removed his helmet and kissed the boy, then prayed to Zeus that the boy might be "a better man than his father."

649–50 *You were named . . . unpierceable oxhide.* The name Eurysakes literally means "broad shield."

674–711 first *stasimon* ("act-dividing" choral song)

712–69 second *episode*

712–59 *Great, unfathomable time . . . a treacherous harbor.* Aias' sudden, unannounced appearance is unusual in extant tragedy. Customarily, characters entering after a choral ode are put into some clear verbal rapport with other characters on stage, either through direct address or choral introduction. The enormous size of, as well as the use of masks in, the Greek theater requires that stage relations between characters be firmly established, often with lengthy verbal introductions. The absence of either introduction or addressee signals the unusual character of the speech.

716 *most dread oath* Oaths were sacred and inviolable, and no less a god than Zeus himself punished those who broke them. Aias swore a "dread oath" when he sailed for Troy: together with the other Greek princes, he swore to protect the honor of the man who married the beautiful Helen. As Teukros states later, Aias only fought for the Atreidai because a great oath bound him (1245).

726 *this filth* "Pollution" was taken very seriously by the Greeks, and represented something far more complicated than our "guilt." It was sometimes as much a god-sent disease (compare the threats made by the Furies at the end of Aeschylus' *Eumenides*, 778 ff.) as the consequence of immoral action. A man could be polluted by a bad dream, contact with death or certain repellent diseases, and by the stain of murder—or that of some other terrible crime—like Aias' here. A polluted man must be ritually purified of the "bad blood" or even, in certain cases of indelible pollution, like that of Oedipus, driven into exile because his pollution might blight land and populace, innocent and guilty alike. Aias' words, however, are ambiguous. The "bathing place" (724), by which Aias implies he seeks purification, is the same expression used later by Teukros to describe the place for washing the dead body (1597, "sacred bath").

734 *took it in gift* In the *Iliad*, the two champions exchanged tokens of honor after their single combat, which ended in a draw as night fell. Hektor proposed the exchange, offering his silver-studded sword in order that, in

his words, "any Achaian or Trojan may say that / we who fought in heart-devouring hate parted joined together as friends" (*Iliad* 7.300–2). Aias, in turn, gave Hektor his purple loin guard.

753–59 *I know now . . . treacherous harbor.* Words like those of the Cynic, Bias (compare Aristotle's *Rhetoric*, 1389b 24–25). This is the unheroic morality, the ethos of contingency, based on the universal uncertainty Aias describes. Similar words spoken by Hektor to Aias in the *Iliad* (see note at 734) come to opposite moral conclusions and even sound, in the heroic context, a note of moral triumph. Compare, however, the moral conclusion drawn by Odysseus, based on Aias' same principle of uncertainty, at the end of the play (1500 ff.).

770–95 second *stasimon*

783 *Rage* The Greek word is Ares, god of war, to whom Aias is often compared by Homer, and here the personification of Aias' anger

796–1330 third *episode*

796–824 *Friends, I have messages . . . know about it?* A messenger bringing news of the hero's death is doubtless what the audience expects, that is a "speech" but not the suicide itself, since acts of violence were never performed on the Greek stage. The spectator often bore witness to the aftermath of violent acts, the spectacle of mortality—a dead body or dying man—but not the monstrous act that caused it. For example, we see the bodies of Agamemnon and Cassandra but not their murder, the fragmentary remains of Pentheus but not his dismemberment, and blood-soaked Aias but not the slaughter of the livestock—awful revelation, not brutal realism. Contrary to expectations, however, this messenger introduces another postponement of the hero's death. Instead of delivering a conventional eyewitness account of the hero's death, the messenger reports what has been "said" about Aias and introduces the possibility that he may survive. Note the stress on what was merely "said" rather than actually "seen," an important distinction in Greek—825, 836, 841 ff., 856 ff., 864, 868.

825–69 *What I heard . . . is no more.* This messenger speech is unusual in several ways. That the messenger's stories are without traditional precedent and that the messenger has them secondhand possibly suggests that his account belongs merely to the realm of "words" and "possibilities"—a realm that Aias has moved beyond.

838–39. *outsized bodies . . . grown / from the human branch* Aias is *perissos*, "huge," "prodigious," "exceptional," a man who exceeds the limits set by nature. The adjective regularly used to describe him in Homer, *pelorios*, "gigantic," is generally used to describe monstrous prodigies, such as the Cyclops, Skylla, or the Gorgon, etc.

841–52 *The man's father . . . without them.*" These two stories appear to be Sophocles' invention, and they set Aias apart from the gods on whom others pin their hopes. Aias prefers his own certain courage to the uncertain gods. In the *Iliad* Aias is not represented as hostile to the gods, though he never figures in their plans or considerations. Unlike other heroes, such as Achilles or Odysseus, Aias had no divine patron.

939–41 *so make them die . . . hands of their dearest / offspring.* Agamemnon did indeed die at the hands of his own wife, but Aias' was not the only curse on his house. The root of his family's afflictions goes back to Tantalos, a mythical son of Zeus, who served the gods a feast of his son Pelops' flesh. However, Menelaos returned home to a charmed life with Helen.

953–57 *O death . . . and never again* These lines are bracketed by many editors, including Lloyd-Jones and Wilson. In general, they object to the strangeness of Aias' addressing the Sun above (945 f.), then invoking Death ("come, death, attend me" [953]) and then, as if he were stalling ("or I will come to you there" [954]), then the Sun a second time. But the sudden shift away from Death and back to the Sun, as well as the pointed invocation of its heavenly light (955), make the surprisingly unconventional association of the suicide with radiance and vision that much more emphatic.

964–65 *The rest / I will . . . in Hades.* Aias' last word in Greek is *mythēsomai*, "I will speak," suggesting perhaps that dead, Aias will enter what Stanford has called a "Communion of Heroes." There is an irony here—and a hint that Sophocles' Aias is being differentiated from the conventional Aias; in Hades Aias was famous above all for his "silence," when his shade refused to speak to Odysseus (*Odyssey* 11.563 ff.).

965 *the dead in Hades.* A thicket of scholarly controversy has grown around the question of how the suicide itself is managed. But most commentators deal only with technical aspects of stagecraft: whether Aias jumps behind a bush or through the stage door, when and how a dummy is substituted for the body, so that the actor playing Aias can, in keeping

with the "three actor rule," reenter to play another part (for a summary of the main arguments, see Gardiner, "The Staging of the Death of Ajax," *The Classical Journal* 1979, 75, 10–14).

966–1058 second *kommos*

994 *Aias is here* Suicide was not morally tainted in Greek, as opposed to Christian, culture, because the Greeks did not regard fate and divine providence as coterminous. Suicide then did not interfere with "God's plan." Aristotle would later describe suicide as an antisocial act, since it deprived the community of a potential productive member. His categories, however, do not really apply to the hero who is always beyond the city in his tragic isolation. But that suicide was not held in heroic honor can be glimpsed in scenes from archaic art, where Aias, the sole "heroic" suicide, is mostly hunched over his sword, hideously gored, prone, or on all fours like a huge beast.

1011–15 *I will wrap him . . . raw / wound* Compare the words spoken by Aeschylus' Tekmessa (from the lost *Women of Salamis*, frg. 216N) upon discovering Aias' body: "If only there were a shroud like heaven." The words of Sophocles' Tekmessa are as visceral as those of Aeschylus' are tinged with transcendence. The image of the impaled Aias that Sophocles conjures here and whose traditional associations he later confounds is one avoided even by Attic vase painters. Once a popular subject in archaic art, the suicide virtually disappears in Attic art from the early sixth century, when Salamis becomes an Athenian possession and Aias an Athenian hero.

1111–12 *that hard face, / that grim self-command!* Aias' fierce face was proverbial. Describing a Hellenistic portrait gallery, the ancient writer Philostratus wrote, "You can recognize Aias by his grim look" (*Imagines* 350). The adjective *blosuros*, "fierce," "grim," used in Homer to describe Aias' face (*Iliad.* 7.212.) is also used of lions, the Gorgon, and of Fear on Herakles' shield in Hesiod.

1122–23 *bastard, / gotten by a hostile spear* On Teukros' genealogy see on lines 473–76.

1129 *I'll be banished* After returning home to Salamis, Teukros went into exile at Cyprus. Aeschylus dealt with this subject in the third play of his Aias trilogy, *The Women of Salamis*. Sophocles also wrote a play about Teukros, dealing with the aftermath of this play. In it, according to Aristotle (*Rhetoric*. 3.15 p. 1416 b1), Odysseus prosecutes Teukros for having abandoned Aias!

1136 f. *bright, biting sword-point* Literally, "a thing that bites." The sword is also personified (908 f.), as if it were a living force. Compare Pindar's description of Envy "biting" Aias "with a sword," *Nemean* 8.23 f. The comparison is worth noting because Sophocles also recalls several other curious details from Pindar's Aias ode in his description of the sword.

1138–46 *Did you see . . . falling on it.* Homer says only that Achilles tied and then dragged Hektor, already dead, behind his chariot, and no mention is made of Aias' loin-guard (*Iliad* 22.361 ff.). Sophocles, however, conceives of Hektor dragged alive and describes the paradoxical link between the two men's fates as though well known (from a lost epic?) to his audience.

1165 ff. MENELAOS enters A heated debate over Aias' burial now follows. The conventional sequence of debate and death has in fact been dramatically reversed. The loss of a great debate/quarrel with Odysseus over Achilles' arms preceded and partially caused Aias' death. Aeschylus presented this debate in his *The Award of the Arms* (frg. 174–78aN), and it appears to have been a popular subject in fourth-century drama and rhetoric. But in Sophocles' play, "debate" is relegated to the aftermath, and turned into a mean-spirited volley of abusive insult.

1165 *hands off that corpse* Just before at 1156, the chorus refers to Aias ("him") specifically as a "man," *anēr*, normally used of the living. Now, to Menelaos, he is a merely a corpse, *nekros*.

1200 *bulwark of fear* Sparta honored Fear itself with a statue. Menelaos is King of Sparta. In the fifth century, Menelaos' emphasis on discipline and fear here make him sound like a fifth-century Spartan.

1245 *oaths he had sworn.* Aias, like the other Greeks who had been Helen's suitors, swore the oath to protect the man who finally married her. Teukros alleges that it was only the sacred oath which brought Aias to Troy. Nothing perhaps better illustrates the fundamental difference between Aias the true aristocrat and Menelaos the autocrat: Aias came under his own sails, bound by his word of honor, not a superior's commands.

1253–54 ff. *The archer / has . . .* The prejudice in favor of spearmen over archers goes back to Homer and continues in fifth-century B.C. literature (e.g., Euripides' *Herakles* 157 ff.). The (democratic) bow was, at least until the battle of Delium (424 B.C.), held in contempt by aristocratic Athenians; it was used by the city police, always barbarian slaves; and was the weapon of the Persians. But Teukros was the greatest of the bowmen in the *Iliad*, and other great archaic heroes, such as Philoctetes and even Herakles himself, were famous bowmen.

1271 *fixed the vote.* The *Odyssey* and epic fragments suggest that, because the Greeks were unable to choose between Odysseus and Aias, Trojan captives were asked to decide the award. The Greek "vote" was possibly introduced by Pindar in his Aias ode, *Nemean* 8 (elsewhere, he also disparages the Greek choice of Odysseus: see *Nemean* 7.23–27 and *Isthmian* 4.36–40); he almost certainly introduced the notion that the voting was "fixed," which he refers to as "something new." Sophocles pointedly recalls the Pindaric variant, partly because his play is a response to the condemnation of Athens implicit in Pindar's ode. The play cannot be dated with certainty (see Introduction, pp. 19 ff.), although public reaction to it has been compared (by Libanius, *Declamatio* 14.20) to that accorded Phrynichus' disturbingly topical *Siege of Miletus*, for which the playwright was allegedly fined.

1278 ff. *I saw a man once . . .* Oblique insults and threats in allegorical form were old, popular types of abuse.

1313 ff. *kneel here* The return of Tekmessa and the child sets the stage for the *tableau vivant* that visually dominates the end of the play. The mourning group has the power of the dead and the inviolability of suppliancy (protected by Zeus) on their side, thereby suggesting that the actions of the Atreidai border on sacrilege.

1331–66 third *stasimon* (see Introduction pp. 21 f.)

1367–1593 fourth *episode*

1410 *than a shadow!* Precisely Odysseus' word in response to the spectacle of Aias fallen ("we who live / are all phantoms, fleeting shadows," 151–52), but spoken now with contempt, not compassion.

1412 *bring someone else . . .* In fifth-century Athens persons not born of free parents were denied the rights of full citizenship and were therefore not entitled to plead their own case. The anachronism is worth noting, and, in general, the pointedness, for contemporary Athenians, of Sophocles' writing.

1419–48 *a man dies . . . barbarian woman's son.* Teukros responds by recalling Aias' greatest Homeric moments in the *Iliad*: his lonely effort to prevent Hektor from firing the Greek ships (15.415 ff.); his single-combat with Hektor (7.38 ff.). Menelaos had volunteered to fight Hektor, but Agamemnon, fearing the outcome, persuaded the Greek champions to draw lots. The lot freely thrown into the helmet by Aias, "the lightest / bit of clay" (1443–45), contrasts sharply with the Greeks' "fixed" voting for the arms (1271).

1455–59 *Your mother . . . speechless fish.* Cretans had a bad reputation in fifth-century Athens for, among other things, dishonesty (see Glossary, CRETAN).

1511–13 *greatest of all . . . to Achilles.* Odysseus confirms the esteem in which Aias is held throughout Homer (*Iliad* 2.768–69; 17.279–80; *Odyssey* 11.550–51; 24.17–18).

1594–1608 *exodos*

1604–5 *while Aias lived . . . man in the world.* Although the meaning is reasonably clear, the text of these lines appears corrupt and no editor has satisfactorily explained them. Teukros' strange, temporal emphasis (even stronger in Greek) on the nobility of Aias "while he lived," though the play has dramatized his greatness in facing death, may be Sophocles' way of separating at the coda the timeless hero from the rest. George Eliot remarked that those who survive the Sophoclean hero go on living "life at the lower end."

1606–8 *Mortals know . . . end will be.* Sophocles ends five of his seven extant plays with choral comment. Modern readers are cautioned against the tendency to look too deeply into these stylized codas. (Euripides uses one particular coda, similar to this, in six of his plays.) Nonetheless, these words contrasting mere sight with vision are appropriate.

GLOSSARY

ACHILLES: son of Peleus and Thetis, the greatest of Greek heroes at Troy. After Agamemnon took away his concubine, Briseis, he refused to fight for the Greeks until the death of his close companion, Patroklos. Returning to battle, he killed Hektor and not long after was himself killed, shot in the heel by the Trojan prince, Paris.

AEGEAN: the sea lying between mainland Greece and Asia Minor.

AGAMEMNON: prince of Mycenae and Argos, son of Atreus and brother of Menelaos. He was elected commander-in-chief of the Greek forces that sailed against Troy. When he returned to Argos after the fall of Troy, he was murdered by his wife Klytemnestra in conspiracy with her adulterer, Aigisthos.

AIAKIDAI: descendants of Aiakos, himself the son of Zeus. They included Telamon, Peleus, Aias, and Teukros.

AIAS (Ajax):   son of Telamon and prince of Salamis. He was a hero of great courage and enormous size, standing head and shoulders above all others at Troy, but traditionally stolid and slow of speech. Second only to Achilles among the Greek warriors, he went mad with anger and finally killed himself when, after Achilles' death, his armor was awarded to Odysseus.

ALKMENE: mortal woman who became by Zeus the mother of the hero Herakles.

APOLLO: god of prophecy, healing, music and lyric poetry, archery and discursive (or forensic) speech, often associated with the higher developments of civilization. As a light-bringing god, he is closely connected with, but distinct from, Helios, god of the sun.

ARES: Greek god of war, to whom Aias is often compared in Homer.

ARTEMIS: Greek virgin goddess of hunting and childbirth.

ATHENE: born of no mother, springing fully armed from the head of Zeus, she was the patron goddess of war (Athene Promachos), credited with inventing the war chariot, and also the patroness of Greek cities (Athene Polias), particularly of Athens, as well as of the arts and handicrafts in general. Among her favorites at Troy were Diomedes and Odysseus.

ATHENS: chief city of Attika and home of Sophocles.

ATREIDAI: Agamemnon and Menelaos, the sons of Atreus.

ATREUS: king of Mycenae, son of Pelops, and father of Agamemnon and Menelaos. He served his brother, Thyestes, a dinner containing the flesh of his children after learning that Thyestes had seduced his wife, Aëropē. After discovering the nature of the dish, Thyestes placed a curse on Atreus' house.

BOSPHORUS: channel in Thrace connecting the Sea of Marmora (Propontis) with the Black Sea.

CRETAN: of Crete, one of the largest islands in the Mediterranean, south of the Cyclades. Cretan Aëropē, Agamemnon's mother, had been caught in adultery by her father, Katreus, and sentenced to death by drowning. However, she was spared by Katreus' friend, Nauplios, and married to Atreus, whom she later betrayed (ATREUS).

DELOS: Cycladic island in the Aegean, birthplace of Apollo and Artemis; an important site in the worship of Apollo and seat of one of his most important oracles.

ENYALIOS: alternate incarnation of Ares.

ERECHTHEUS: a famous king of Athens, a son of Earth reared by Athena, with whom he was often honored.

ERIBOIA: wife of Telamon and mother of Aias.

EURYSAKES: son of Aias and Tekmessa.

FURIES: the three female ministers of divine vengeance, born from the blood of Ouranos when he was castrated by his son Kronos.

HADES: lord of the underworld, frequently equated with his own kingdom.

HEKTOR: son of Priam and Hecuba, and bravest of all the Trojans who fought against the Greeks. After killing Patroklos, he himself was finally killed by Achilles, who dragged his body behind a chariot to the Greek camp and then around Patroklos' tomb.

HELIOS: Greek personification of the sun, conceived of as a charioteer who daily drives from east to west across the sky.

HERAKLES: son of Zeus by the mortal woman Alkmene, and the most renowned of all Greek heroes.

HERMES: god of heralds, travelers, thieves, inventor of the lyre, and messenger of the gods. It was his function to escort the souls of the dead to the lower world.

ICARIAN: of Icaria, a small island in the Aegean.

IDA: mountain or ridge of mountains near Troy, site of the Judgment of Paris and the source of several rivers, including Simois and Skamander.

KALCHAS: a celebrated soothsayer, he accompanied the Greeks to Troy as their high priest.

KNOSIAN: of Knossos, principal city of Crete and famous for its dances.

KYLLENE: a mountain in the Peloponnissos, site of the birth of Hermes.

LAERTES: king of Ithaka, he married Antiklea who bore him Odysseus. According to another tradition, Antiklea was already pregnant by Sisyphos with Odysseus when she married Laertes.

LAOMEDON: Trojan king, father of Priam and Hesione. With the aid of Apollo and Poseidon, he built the walls of Troy. When refused payment, the two gods brought destructive forces against the city; these forces could only be appeased by the annual offer of a young Trojan woman to a sea monster. When the annual lot fell to Laomedon's daughter, Hesione, he made a bargain with Herakles to destroy the monster. When Herakles completed his task, Laomedon refused to reward him, whereupon Herakles, with the aid of Telamon, besieged Troy.

MENELAOS: prince of Sparta, son of Atreus and brother of Agamemnon. He urged the Greeks to honor the oaths they had sworn to protect his wife, Helen, when she was abducted by Paris.

MYSIAN: of Mysia, region in Asia Minor, where the Phrygian Great Mother Goddess, Cybele (often identified by Greeks with Zeus' mother, Rhea, and cult-companion of Pan) was widely worshiped.

ODYSSEUS: prince of Ithaka, the husband of Penelope and father of Telemachos. A central figure in the *Odyssey*, which narrates his ten years of wandering after the fall of Troy and his eventual return home to his kingdom. Represented by Homer as both brave and wise, he is increasingly portrayed by later authors, especially the tragedians, as a cunning, deceitful, and extremely articulate demagogue.

OLYMPOS: highest mountain on the Greek peninsula, separating Macedonia from Thessaly, and traditional home of the gods.

PAN: half goat and half man; the god of shepherds, often portrayed as chief of the satyrs.

PELOPS: son of Tantalos. He won Hippodamia as his wife by defeating her father, king Oenomaus, in a chariot race, which was won by bribing the king's driver to remove the linchpin of the chariot. By having the driver thrown into the sea instead of rewarding him, Pelops brought down a curse on his house, a curse that descended to his sons, Atreus and Thyestes.

PHRYGIAN: of Phrygia, country in the interior of Asia Minor.

SALAMIS: an island in the Saronic gulf separated by a narrow channel from the western coast of Attika. It was the ancient home of Telamon, Aias, and Teukros and the site of the crushing defeat of the Persian fleet by the Greeks in 480 B.C. Athens took possession of it as a deme in the early sixth century.

SISYPHOS: son of Aeolus and the most crafty prince of the heroic age. He slept with Antiklea, the daughter of his neighbor Autolykos, a few days before her marriage to Laertes, thereby rendering the paternity of her son Odysseus doubtful. For crimes unknown, Sisyphos in Hades was eternally condemned to roll a giant boulder up a steep hill, only to have it always roll back down again. Odysseus' enemies alleged that Sisyphos was his true father.

SKAMANDER: one of the principal rivers of the Troad, rising in Mount Ida and flowing into the Hellespont.

SPARTANS: men of Sparta, chief city in the extreme south of the Peloponnissos and, in the fifth century, Athens' greatest enemy.

TEKMESSA: daughter of the Phrygian prince, Teleutas. She became the consort of Aias and mother of his son, Eurysakes, after Aias killed her father in war.

TELAMON: king of Salamis, father of Aias by Eriboia, his wife, and of Teukros by Hesione, his concubine.

TELEUTAS: prince of Phrygia and father of Tekmessa, killed in battle by Aias.

TEUKROS: son of Telamon by Hesione and half-brother of Aias. He was best archer among the Greeks who came to Troy. Absent at the time of Aias' suicide, he returned to secure his burial. Banished by his father upon returning home, he went to Cyprus, where he founded a new town of Salamis.

TROY: city on the northern coast of Asia Minor founded by Dardanos. Under its king, Priam, it was besieged and finally, after ten years of struggle, taken by an expedition of Greeks who came to recapture Helen, wife of Menelaos, who had been abducted to Troy by Paris, son of Priam.

ZEUS: chief god of the Greek pantheon.